Enhancing Fashion E-
The Power of Advar

By
SUDHA MISRA

TABLE OF CONTENTS

CHAPTER NO.	TITLE	PAGE NO.
	LIST OF TABLES	
	LIST OF FIGURES	
	LIST OF ABBREVIATIONS	
	ABSTRACT	
1	**INTRODUCTION**	1
	1.1 BACKGROUND	1
	1.1.1 Understanding the concept of E-commerce	1
	1.1.2 Basic functioning of operations through E-Commerce	3
	1.1.3 Classification of Electronic commerce	3
	1.1.4 E-Commerce - Market share	5
	1.1.5 Evolution of E-Commerce in India	5
	1.1.6 Key drivers in Indian e-commerce	6
	1.1.7 Indian E-commerce: Market size and growth	7
	1.2 RATIONALE FOR RESEARCH	8
	1.3 SCOPE OF THE RESEARCH	10
	1.4 PURPOSE OF THE RESEARCH	11
	1.5 DEFINITIONS AND TERMINOLOGIES USED	13
	1.6 DELIMITATIONS OF THE SCOPE AND KEY ASSUMPTIONS	14
	1.7 OUTLINE OF THESIS	15

CHAPTER NO.		TITLE	PAGE NO.
2		**REVIEW OF LITERATURE**	17
	2.1	COMMUNICATION BETWEEN THE BUYER AND THE SELLER IN DISTANCE BUYING	17
	2.2	TRENDS IN APPAREL AND LIFESTYLE SHOPPING	19
	2.3	TREMENDOUS ECONOMIC VALUE	21
	2.4	YOUNGER DEMOGRAPHIC	24
	2.5	INTERNET USERS	24
	2.6	RISE OF MOBILE COMMERCE	26
	2.7	ECOMMERCE MARKET IN INDIA	27
	2.8	BLENDING VIDEO AND ECOMMERCE	27
	2.9	STUDY ON RETURNS	33
	2.10	REASONS FOR RETURNS	42
	2.11	SUMMARY	48
3		**METHODOLOGY**	51
	3.1	INTRODUCTION	51
	3.2	PRIMARY RESEARCH	53
		3.2.1 Primary Data	53
		3.2.1.1 Data collected from study at e-commerce Industry	53
		3.2.1.2 Data collected through questionnaire	53
		3.2.1.3 Interviews with Industry Experts	55.
		3.2.1.4 Data collected by study at offline stores	55

CHAPTER NO.		TITLE	PAGE NO.
		3.2.1.5 Data collected by Studying and experiencing various online stores	55
	3.3	SECONDARY RESEARCH	55
		3.3.1 Secondary Data	56
		3.3.1.1 Studied and data collected for various websites	56
4		**DATA ANALYSIS**	57
	4.1	INTRODUCTION	57
	4.2.	ANALYSIS OF DATA COLLECTED THROUGH QUESTIONNAIRE	57
		4.2.1 Correlation between various attributes	67
		4.2.1.1. The correlation between the attributes and their impact where people shifted from online buying to offline buying in the last six months.	67
		4.2.1.2 The correlation between the attributes and their impact where people shifted from offline to online shopping of apparel.	68
		4.2.1.3 The correlation between the attributes and their impact on people, who shop online.	69
		4.2.1.4 Summary	70

CHAPTER NO.			TITLE		PAGE NO.
	4.3	ANALYSIS OF OFFLINE STUDY DONE AT VARIOUS BRICK AND MORTAR STORES			72
		4.3.1.	Identification of attributes to the problem of size and fit		72
		4.3.2.	Summary		75
	4.4	ANALYSIS OF THE STUDY DONE AT FLIPKART			76
	4.5	ANALYSIS OF STUDY DONE WITH VARIOUS ECOMMERCE COMPANIES			78
		4.5.1	Study at Snapdeal		78
		4.5.2	Study at Fashionara		79
		4.5.3	Study at 100bestbuy		80
		4.5.4	Study at Myntra		80
	4.6	SUMMARY OF THE STUDY			81
5	**RECOMMENDATIONS**				**82**
	5.1	SIZE AND FIT			82
		5.1.1	New size chart		82
		5.1.2	Design thinking		84
			5.1.2.1	Creative Ideas	85
			5.1.2.2	A garment is designed and fully constructed as part of this research	88
			5.1.2.3	Testing of the garment created	90
		5.1.3	Online trial room		90
			5.1.3.1	Recommended software application	
			5.1.3.2	Application Development	94
			5.1.3.3	Working of Virtual fitting room	103

CHAPTER NO.		TITLE	PAGE NO.
		5.1.3.4 Summary	108
	5.2	COLOUR SOLUTION	109
		5.2.1 Understanding the importance of colour	109
		5.2.2 Solutions to Colour complications	109
		5.2.2.1 Pantone colour matching system	109
		5.2.2.2 Implementation of Pantone code	110
	5.3	PRODUCT DESCRIPTION	113
		5.3.1 Introduction	113
		5.3.2 The important attributes to describe a garment are mentioned below	114
		5.3.2.1 Material	114
		5.3.2.2. Recommendation for indication of fabric thickness	115
		5.3.2.3 Length of the garment	117
		5.3.2.4 Wash Care	117
		5.3.2.5 Return Policy	117
		5.3.2.5 Delivery time	117
		5.3.2.6 View of the garment	118
		5.3.3 Use of video technology	118
6		**CONCLUSIONS AND FUTURE WORK**	**122**
	6.1	CONCLUSIONS	122
	6.2	FUTURE WORK	123
		6.2.1 Video Commerce	123
		6.2.2 HAPTICS	125

LIST OF TABLES

TABLE NO.	TITLE	PAGE NO.
Table 1.1	Classification of E-Commerce	4
Table 1.2	Terminologies and Abbreviation in E-Commerce	14
Table 4.1	Male and female in each age category	58
Table 4.2	Problem areas in Women's top-wear	73
Table 4.3	Problem areas in women's wear Kurta category	74
Table 4.4	Major Reasons for Return	76
Table 4.5	Reasons for return at 100bestbuy	80
Table 4.6	Summary of the study	81
Table 5.1	Size chart for women's wear top	83
Table 5.2	Size chart with all the important attributes	84
Table 5.3	Size chart for size Medium with chest 40 inches and all waist combinations from 35 inches to 43 inches	94
Table 5.4	Database for size Medium with chest 40 and all the combinations for the waist from 30 inches to 40 inches along with the images clicked for the front and the back side of the garment	96
Table 5.5	Database for size Medium with chest 39 and all the combinations for the waist from 28 inches to 40 inches along with the images clicked for the front and the back side of the garment	97
Table 5.6	Database for size Medium with chest 38 and all the combinations for the waist from 28 inches to 39 inches along with the images clicked for the front and the back side of the garment	98

TABLE NO.	TITLE	PAGE NO.
Table 5.7	Database for size Medium with chest 37 and all the combinations for the waist from 28 inches to 36 inches along with the images clicked for the front and the back side of the garment	99
Table 5.8	Database for size Medium with chest 36 and all the combinations for the waist from 28 inches to 36 inches along with the images clicked for the front and the back side of the garment	100
Table 5.9	Database for size Medium with chest 35 and all the combinations for the waist from 28 inches to 34 inches along with the images clicked for the front and back side of the garment	101
Table 5.10	Database for size Medium with chest 34 and all the combinations for the waist from 28 inches to 33 inches along with the images clicked for the front and the back side of the garment	102

LIST OF FIGURES

FIGURE NO.	TITLE	PAGE NO.
Figure 1	Basic functioning of E-commerce operations	3
Figure 3.1	Methodology	52
Figure 4.1	Male and female in various age groups	58
Figure 4.2	Reasons for shopping from a physical store	59
Figure 4.3	Shopping preference based on occupation	60
Figure 4.4	Customers preference for online shopping	61
Figure 4.5	Attributes people consider while buying apparel online	62
Figure 4.6	Reasons for return	63
Figure 4.7	Factors influence online shopping	64
Figure 4.8	Attributes to make online shopping better and improved	65
Figure 4.9	Video describing the garment creation helps in understanding garment better	66
Figure 4.10	Preference for virtual fitting solution	67
Figure 4.11	Problem areas in women's top-wear in a physical store	73
Figure 4.12	Problem areas women's wear straight kurta in a physical store	74
Figure 4.13	Major problem areas in Flipkart	77
Figure 4.14	Reasons for return in Snapdeal	78
Figure 4.15	Reasons for return in Fashionara	79
Figure 5.1	Kimono sleeves	85
Figure 5.2	Kaftan Sleeve	86
Figure 5.3	Raglan sleeves	86
Figure 5.4	Drop Shoulder short sleeves	87

FIGURE NO.	TITLE	PAGE NO.
Figure 5.5	Specifications of the front and back of the garment created	88
Figure 5.6	Front and back side of the top with adjustable button	89
Figure 5.7	Adjustable buttons at the back side of the top provided with 3 options to adjust the fit	89
Figure 5.8	Actual garment without closing the adjustable buttons and with closed buttons	90
Figure 5.9	Recommended virtual fitting Algorithm	93
Figure 5.11	Front page of actual application	103
Figure 5.12	Measurement page of the actual application	104
Figure 5.13	Measurement page with proceed button	104
Figure 5.14	Fit advice as per the body measurements given	105
Figure 5.15	Fit advice if chosen size is 40.	106
Figure 5.16	Fit advice if chosen size is 42	106
Figure 5.17	Fit advice if chosen size is 44	107
Figure 5.18	Pantone code colour swatch	111
Figure 5.19	Recommended Solution with implemented pantone cod	112
Figure 5.20	Garments with all the available colours can be shown on the same page	113
Figure 5.21	An example of description	115
Figure 5.22	Thickness Guide	116
Figure 5.23	Views of the garments to be shown for a garment	118
Figure 5.24	The video of the garment can be shown on the description page.	119
Figure 5.25	video link: https://youtu.be/GODT_CljmqE	120
Figure 5.26	A shot from the video made where an expert is describing the garment	121

LIST OF ABBREVIATIONS

Abbreviations

EC	Electronic Commerce
B2B	Business to Business
B2C	Business to Consumer
B2B2C	Business to Business to Consumer
B2E	Business to Employee
C2B	Consumer to Business
C2C	Consumer to Consumer
C-Commerce	Collaborative Commerce
GDP	Gross Domestic Product
IAMAI	Internet And Mobile Association Of India
GST	Goods and Services Tax
E-Marketers	Electronic Marketers
SRS	Technique Simple Random Sampling
E-Mannequin	Electronic Mannequin
CMYK	Cyan Magenta Yellow Black
E-commerce/e-commerce	Electronic commerce
M-commerce	Mobile Commerce/Purchasing from mobile
E-shopping	Electronic shopping from web site
e-Store/online/virtual store	Online Store

E-Tail	Electronic Retail
CAGR	Compound Annual Growth Rate
GSM	Grams per Square Meter
	(Metric measurement of the weight of a fabric)
VTR	View Through Rate
SEO	Search Engine Optimisation
HTML	Hyper Text Markup Language
TV	Television
IT	Information Technology
COD	Cash On Delivery
3D	3Dimensional
CD	Compact Disc
EMI	Equated Monthly Installment
IMRB	Indian Market Research Bureau

ABSTRACT

The main objective of this research is to envisage recommendations to address the problematic areas in the apparel e-commerce and to drive the businesses such that they are able to elevate the overall customer experience and to reduce the problem of rampant returns thereby directly contributing to the bottom line of apparel e-commerce. This research also offers a virtual fit software solution to help the customers in choosing the right size and fit for the garment.

A study was done with Flipkart, one of the leading e-commerce companies to understand the problem of returns. Based on the return data collected from online customers, considering geographical proximity as Bangalore and the age group between 18 and 35years, the data size was formed as 1000. The data was collected via a questionnaire filled by apparel online customers. The final data size was 891.The analysis has been done using "R" software. Various correlations were done to find the odds ratio to compare the impact of various attributes with respect to online shopping.

Data was also collected by observation at various offline stores to understand the sizing and the fit issues. Secondary research was done to understand the structure and dynamics of digital commerce market place in India. A data validation check was performed from information retrieved from various articles, corporate reports, newspaper articles and white papers.

The questionnaire analysis showed that 42% of fashion apparel is returned because of the problem of size and fit, 19% were because of fabric quality problem and 8% were because of colour problem. The correlation between variables such as the shift from online to offline shopping in the last six months highlights the inability of customer to check for size and fit while shopping online. 67% of online shoppers also had a suggestion that if the fit of the garment could be visualized i.e. virtual fitting solution, it would help in selecting the legitimately fitted garment.

According to the research conducted by various researchers, 23% of all clothes purchased online are returned. According to the study conducted by Forbes in 2011, the customers that purchase the garment find that their best guess for size was imprecise after they tried the garment received. About 70% of garments are returned because the garment did not fit as the customer expected.

The data for this research was also collected via personal interviews of the top key executives of some of the largest e-commerce companies in India, and according to them, the returns percentage ranged from 12% to 25%. From the analysis of data, it is quite clear that both the customer experience and the profitability of the fashion e-commerce companies take a substantial toll due to the clear problems categorised into three broad areas:

a. Size and fit

b. Colour

c. Product description

The scope of this research is to envisage recommendations to address these problematic areas. The proposed recommendations in the above areas can assist customers to purchase apparel online and will offer them the same experience in selecting a garment as offline purchase. The suggested virtual fitting solution can also help customers to virtually try the garment and assure themselves of the fit and has the potential to reduce returns. This benefits both the consumer and the producer.

CHAPTER 1

INTRODUCTION

This chapter presents both a theoretical and a practical background of the research field that demarcates the research areas and justifies the purpose of this research. The research questions have also been addressed. The first section concludes with a brief overview of the thesis.

1.1 BACKGROUND

1.1.1 Understanding the concept of E-commerce

The digital world is growing globally and India is no exception. Internet has become very popular in advanced and developing nations alike. The emergence and widespread adoption of computers and the World Wide Web in late nineties has once again led to changes in business practices with commerce occurring over the Internet. Internet is moving from fixed access to ubiquitous access. No longer limited to developed markets, it is growing by leaps and bounds in emerging markets. These markets are increasingly driving innovation. No matter what stage their industry is currently in, it is time for them to start their e-commerce activities. If they wait they will miss the opportunity (Martin, 2001).

Electronic commerce provides the capability of buying and selling products and information on the Internet. As technology is advancing, the lifestyle of urban population is changing, there is also a change in the buying patterns. People are choosing to buy online rather than going to physical stores. The change is observed to a great extent with the millennials - A generation born after 1980s. This generation is often equipped with customer technology like laptops and smart phones (KPMG and IAMAI, 2013).

Due to highly urbanised living culture, people do not suffice the time to go to a store physically to browse and shop. The commute in grid-locked metropolitan cities is not conducive to relaxed shopping, with stores scattered around high-density areas of the city. Further, the Tier-II cities of India do not have the infrastructure or access to physical stores that provides both value for money and contemporary design. Hi-speed bandwidth and improved quality of screens on smart phones is helping this explosive growth in adoption of e-commerce. The government and regulatory bodies are also playing their part by investing in infrastructure and policy support. These bodies have also initiated awareness drives to get wider users (including SMEs/ MSMEs) on to the e-commerce bandwagon (IAMAI-IMRB Digital Commerce report, 2015).

By sitting at one place the customer can explore all the options available in the market and even compare in terms of price and design options.

In apparel e-commerce the customers have to understand design, fabric material, sizes available, colour choices and so on. They need to realise the fit as no two human bodies are similar. The experience of buying fashion needs to be richer than how other categories such as media products viz. books, music and videos or electronics are bought. The customers want shopping experience to be as real as buying from an offline store. There is a lot of technological advancement happening in this area to enhance the online shopping experience.

1.1.2 Basic functioning of operations through E-Commerce

The functioning of the E-commerce operations can be illustrated as in Figure 1.

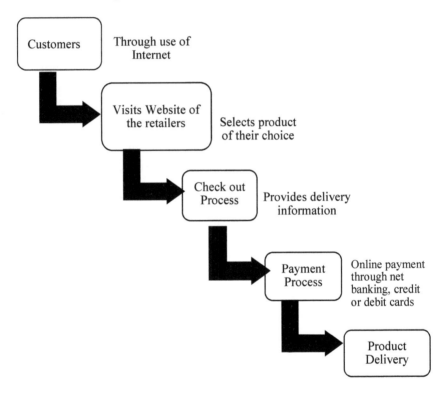

Figure 1 Basic functioning of E-commerce operations

1.1.3 Classification of Electronic commerce

The different E-commerce operations can be classified as in Table 1 below based on their transactions.

Table 1.1 Classification of E-Commerce

Type	Explanation
Business-to-Business (B2B)	The E-commerce model in which the transactions are between the businesses or other organizations.
Business-to-consumer (B2C)	The E-commerce model in which businesses transact with individual Customers. Online-retailing, also termed as e-tailing falls in this category.
Business-to Business-to-consumer (B2B2C)	The E-commerce model in which a business offers product or service to its business client that has its own customers.
Business-to-Employees (B2E)	The E-commerce model in which an organization delivers services, information, or products to its own individual employees.
Consumer-to-Business (C2B)	The E-commerce model in which individuals use the internet to sell products or services to organizations or individuals who seek sellers to bid on products or services they require.
Consumer-to-Consumer (C2C)	The E-commerce model in which the consumers sell their products directly to other consumers.
Intra business EC	The E-commerce that includes all internal activities of the organisation that involves exchange of goods, services, or information among various units and individuals within the organization.
Collaborative-commerce(C-Commerce)	The E-commerce model in which individuals or groups communicate or collaborate online

1.1.4 E-Commerce - Market share

E-commerce business-to-consumer product sales total $142.5 billion, representing about 8% of retail product sales in the United States (Score, 2010). The $26 billion worth of clothes sold online represented about 13% of the domestic market (Forrester, 2011), and as per National retail federation survey, the e-commerce has become one of the most popular cross-shopping (browsing and buying online) methods with 72% of women looking online for apparel purchase. The popularity of online shopping continues to erode sales of conventional retailers. For example, Best Buy, the largest retailer of electronics in the U.S. in August 2014, reported its tenth consecutive quarterly dip in sales, citing an increasing shift by consumers towards online shopping (News, 2014). In 2012, it was seen that about 242 million people had shopped online in China (Xinhuanet, 2013).

1.1.5 Evolution of E-Commerce in India

The Internet wave was started in India in 1995, which was witnessed by the setting up of B2B portals, matrimonial sites, job search directories and online stores through Rediff.com and Indiatimes.com. However, these smaller initiatives did not thrive due to several factors, such as:

- Low Internet penetration
- Slow speed Internet
- Small user base for online shopping
- Inadequate logistics infrastructure
- Low consumer acceptance of e-commerce
- Lack of a tangible revenue model.

More than a thousand e-commerce businesses collapsed due to the

IT downturn in 2000. In the year 2007, a large number of start-ups like Flipkart, Infi-beam, Myntra and Snapdeal stepped into the Indian e-commerce market to make it a vast market. These portals became popular through their rigorous marketing and also by offering services to satisfy the customers and through heavy discounts.

It was seen that India's e-commerce market was worth about $2.5 billion in 2009. It grew up to $6.3 billion in 2011 and further increased to $16 billion in 2013. Market is expected to grow as much as $56 billion by 2023, which will be 6.5% of the total retail market, as quoted by e-Marketer. A major growth in online shopping was witnessed since the introduction of cash on delivery (COD) and free return options followed by availability and affordability of smartphone by majority of Indians (Dudhwewala, 2014).

1.1.6 Key drivers in Indian e-commerce

- Large percentage of population subscribed to broadband Internet, expanding 3G internet users, and a recent introduction of 4G in few cities (IAMAI, 2015).

- Explosive growth of smartphone users, rising standards of living as a result of fast decline in poverty rate, Rapidly promising middle class with better disposable income, especially for travel, electronics and clothing (Analytica, 2015).

- Hectic lifestyles and traffic congestion in urban areas, impacts the attractiveness of conventional shopping thereby providing way for e-commerce, that offers lower prices than in retail outlets.

- Availability of much wider product range (including long tail and Direct Imports) compared to that available at brick and mortar retailers and are challenging in local stores, particularly in tier two and three cities (Analytica, 2015).

- Competitive prices compared to brick and mortar retail, driven by disintermediation and reduced inventory and real estate costs.

- Increased usage of online classified sites and increase in the number of consumers' buying and selling second-hand goods, Cash-on-delivery has been one of the key growth drivers and is flaunted to have accounted for about 50% to 80% of online retail sales (Devmantra, 2015).

- Evolution of E-commerce start-ups like Flipkart, Snapdeal, Amazon India, AJIO, ABOF, Myntra, Saavn, Makemytrip, Bookmyshow, Zomato Etc. have paved way for a tremendous growth in Indian e-commerce Industry (Devmantra, 2015).

1.1.7 Indian E-commerce: Market size and growth

India had its internet user base of about 354 million as of June 2015. As per the study conducted by Subhash and Suryawanshi in March 2017, in the area of E-commerce in India – Challenges and opportunities, E-commerce in India is growing at an astounding rate and is expected to account for 1.61% of the global GDP by 2018 (Suryawanshi, 2017). According to a report by Forrester, India is the fastest growing market in the Asia-pacific region with a growth rate of over 57% between 2012 and 2016. Despite being the second-largest user base in world, only behind China (650 million, 48% of population), the **penetration** of **e-commerce** is low compared to markets like the **United States** (266 million, 84%), or **France** (54 M, 81%), but is growing at an unprecedented rate, adding around 6 million new entrants every month. The industry consensus is that growth is at an inflection point (Vccircle, 2010).

Though, there has been failures in the e-commerce sites for various reasons, and had shut down or were eventually acquired in a misery sale; experts still believe that the Indian e-commerce industry is nowhere near maturity and is expected to have 7% share of the country's retail market by 2023, amounting to $60 billion.

1.2 RATIONALE FOR RESEARCH

The objectives of this research are as follows:

a. To identify main challenges associated with fashion apparel sold via e-commerce.

b. To propose solutions taking into account, the advancements in information technology to resolve the challenges identified and improve the customer experience.

The main challenge is to identify the important factors causing returns in an online apparel business. A study by GSI Commerce reported 69% of respondents as saying that being unable to try on clothes before buying deter them from making fashion purchases online. According to Fits.me, the bricks-and-mortar sales model for fashion apparel is simple: customers try first, and then they buy. On the other hand, the online process is fundamentally the complete opposite: customers must buy first, and only when the garment lands on their doorstep can they eventually try.

In the second instance, having convinced customers to buy clothes online it is also difficult to convince them to keep those clothes: up to 1-in-4 garments bought online are returned. According to research released by Body Labs, a company that uses technology to collect and organize information about human body shapes, poses and movement, 23% of all clothing purchased online is returned. Another 22% of apparel purchased in-store is returned. Another issue that is specific to apparel is fit and sizing. In 2015, $62.4 billion worth of apparel and footwear was returned due to incorrect sizing (IAMAI and KPMG, 2015).

In Lieu of the factors driving the industry and the success of the online-business, organisations across all the industries look at the options of selling their products online. Apparel business is no exception. The apparels are sold online using a web portal. Buying fashion apparel online is very simple with consumers having wide choice of designs to choose from. The operations of the apparel E-commerce are such that the consumers check the descriptions, view pictures of the garment, check the size and make the best guess of the size that suits them and make an order.

On receiving the order when people try the actual garment they may find problem with the size or the fit. Sometimes the problem could be the colour of the apparel or the quality or the product is not the same as ordered. The customers have to understand the apparel design, fabric material, sizes available, colour choices etc. They need to guess the right fit since no two human bodies are similar. The experience of buying fashion needs to be richer than how other categories such as media products viz. books, music and videos or electronics are bought. The customers want shopping experience to be as real as buying from an offline store. There is a lot of technological advancement happening in this area to make apparel buying experience as good as offline.

According to GSI Commerce's study which indicates that if fashion retailers are unable to provide an intuitive online shopping experience, coupled with flexible collection and delivery options, they might face the risk of potential customers deserting them in favour of rival websites.

The majority of factors that stop people from buying clothes or accessories online relate to being unable to physically touch and try on items in order to assess the size, fit, colour and quality of the Garments.

According to research conducted by Body Labs, 23% of all clothing purchased online is returned. Another 22% of apparel purchased offline is also returned.

Another issue that is specific to apparel is fit and sizing. In 2015, $62.4 billion worth of apparel and footwear were returned due to incorrect sizing, according to Body Labs. An upgrade that allowed an e-commerce site gathers more customer information to deliver apparel better suited to the customer would help.

1.3 SCOPE OF THE RESEARCH

Fashion needs to be sold on its craft and its unique point of view needs to come out clearly. Most fashion e-commerce players sell the same merchandise that is being sold in offline channels without much imagination. Essentially, they all end up looking similar and compete purely on price.

From the analysis of data, it is quite clear that both the customer experience and the profitability of the fashion e-commerce companies takes a substantial hit because of clear problems in three broad areas:

    a. Size and fit

    b. Colour

    c. Product description

The scope of the research is to envisage new solutions to address these problematic areas and to drive the business, such that it is able to enhance the customer experience and in reducing the problem of returns thereby directly contributing to the bottom line of fashion apparel e-commerce companies.

1.4 PURPOSE OF THE RESEARCH

The main aim of the thesis is to provide solutions to the following questions:

- Does the fashion garment that can be sold online be manufactured or sized differently?
- How can the garment's USP be communicated to the consumer using advancements in IT so that it helps offset need for touch and feel?
- How can e-commerce companies substitute the experience of fitting trial room?

The research will also provide answers to the following presumptions:

- E-commerce can be very viable proposition for the fashion Apparel Industry.
- To do so, however, fashion e-commerce companies must provide the same services and functions that brick-and-mortar stores provide to meet their customer's needs.
- The use of information technology for technological innovation can provide a dynamic solution to e-commerce industry in their efforts to capture significant share of Apparel market digitally.

- Fashion needs to be more personalized; there needs to be a dialogue, rather than the apparel industry's standard of working always in historical way and on established calendar.

- Fashion needs to be sold on its craft and its unique point of view needs to come out clearly.

- Most e-commerce players sell the same merchandise that is being sold in offline channels without much imagination. Essentially, the Apparel end up looking similar and compete purely on price and in India distinguish only in the area of fulfillment.

- Selling fashion needs a much deeper understanding of kind of merchandise that lends itself to be sold online.

- The garment that can be sold online on long term sustainable basis needs to be uniquely curated than what sells offline as it needs to offset qualities of touch, feel and ornateness.

- A virtual fitting solution can support customer's need to choose the right fit for them, which is not as simple as descriptions, or numbers, or sizing.

- It is an emotional decision about which size someone perceives as looking good on them. Some people want to wear a particular shirt closely fitted, while another person may want to wear the same shirt but wear it larger

- A visual demonstration of fit is possible

- A unique way to show how a certain size will look on their body type is the only way to give shoppers the confidence they need to purchase.

- Secured on the knowledge, the customers are unlikely to need to return the garment for reasons of 'fit'.

Through the thesis, the researcher has attempted to address the problems faced by the customers related to fit, colour, understanding of the apparel and has aimed to provide solutions for the same. This will also examine the correlation between the returns and customer satisfaction and the chief reasons for returns and how various online companies can handle this problem with apparel ecommerce.

Through the thesis, the researcher has attempted to provide solutions to the problems identified in the research in various attributes of apparel ecommerce. The Industry can benefit by incorporating the solutions provided, which will lead to better buying experience for the customers, thereby developing and maintaining loyal customer base. Unless the incidence of returns is addressed, the cost of returns will grow disproportionately despite the issues around sizing. Online clothing sales are expected to grow faster than offline clothing sales.

1.5 DEFINITIONS AND TERMINOLOGIES USED

E-commerce is a more formal and digitally enabled business transaction between the organisations and the individuals (Laudon, 2014).

E-Commerce can also be broadly defined and not restricted to the process of buying and selling of goods and services, but also includes servicing the customers, collaborating with business partners, performing e-learning and managing electronic transactions within the organisation (Turban et al., 2010).

The different terminologies used in the concept of E-commerce are shown in the Table 2 below.

Table 2 Terminologies and Abbreviation in E-Commerce

Sl.No	Full Name	Abbreviated Name/ Complementary Names
1	Electronic- retail	e-tailing
2	Electronic Shopping	e-shopping
3	Online store	e-web store, e-shop, e-store, Internet shop, web shop, web store, online store, online storefront, virtual store
4	Mobile Commerce (purchasing from mobile device)	m-commerce
5	Electronic Commerce	E-Commerce / e-commerce

"Customer" and "consumer" are used interchangeably in the thesis as terms for the end-user, i.e. the one who purchases; however, this individual does not have to be the one who finally consumes the resources.

Return percentages for units are calculated as described below:

$$\text{Return percentage units} = \frac{\text{Returned number of units}}{\text{Delivered number of units}} \quad (1.1)$$

1.6 DELIMITATIONS OF THE SCOPE AND KEY ASSUMPTIONS

The Delimitations of the scope of the research are

- The study is limited to focus on problems of colour, size, fit and description of the apparel.
- The study is done with millennials in the age group of 18 to 30.

- The study is done with the stakeholders of online apparel companies in Bengaluru, although they come in the top 5 apparel companies like Flipkart, Myntra, ABOF, Jabong and so on.

Since the buying apparel online is picking up in India, the touch and feel of the fabric area has been going through a lot of research. Use of Haptics when shopping via smartphones is suggested as a possible solution of future to communicate texture of the fabric. The sensory features of a smartphone such as vibration and audio feedback could be included to enrich the user experience by recreating important dimensions of human tactile perception such as roughness or friction.

It has been assumed that the feedback given by customers in the form of questionnaire were true and the people interviewed during offline study answered truthfully.

1.7 OUTLINE OF THESIS

The section presents a brief outline of the thesis as an introductory guide for the reader. Further, the thesis is organized as follows:

Chapter 2: Literature Review

In this section, the theoretical framework of reference is provided. The previous study in the related field has been supported and its relation with the current study has been established. The existing body of research work and how experts are addressing the problems faced by customers related to fit, colour, and understanding of apparel have been reviewed. It examines main causes of returns in apparels in existing research. It also examines the correlation between the returns and customer satisfaction and the chief reasons for returns and how various online companies are handling this problem.

Chapter 3: Methodology

This section describes the methodology of the research. It enumerates the secondary data available and primary research data collected by questionnaire filled by customers buying apparel online, by in-depth interviews conducted with stakeholders of the e-commerce industry in Bengaluru and by data collected by observation at various offline stores.

Chapter 4: Data Analysis

This section describes the analysis of the data collected and the interpretation of results. It identifies the key challenges associated with apparel ecommerce.

Chapter 5: Recommendations

This section presents the work on modeling and proposing recommendations to the core problem areas uncovered by the analysis of the data.

Chapter 6: Conclusions and future work

This section concludes the thesis and discusses future research directions.

CHAPTER 2

REVIEW OF LITERATURE

In this chapter, the previous studies that are related to apparel ecommerce were examined. Especially, return issues in apparel were focused to identify the relevant variables to be used in this study. Color problems were also studied and the latest innovations happening in apparel ecommerce were also studied and reviewed.

2.1 COMMUNICATION BETWEEN THE BUYER AND THE SELLER IN DISTANCE BUYING

When a company offers its products on distance from the customers, the traditional face-to-face communication has to be replaced by other ways of communicating. According to (Axelsson, 2008) in his research paper "Exploring Relationships between Products Characteristics and B2C Interaction in Electronic Commerce" He has written about communication requirements in electronic commerce based on the type of product, the customer is buying. If a customer wants to order a blue velvet skirt on Internet but she is not sure whether the color is exactly the nuance she is looking for. And how about the fabric, is the textile really as smooth as it looks on the screen? Will "medium" be the right size or should she order "large" instead? A couple of blocks away, another customer is about to order a music-CD on

Internet. He has found a CD of his favorite singer, which he has been searching for a long time. Now he just has to place the order and wait for the delivery.

In this simple example of two distance selling (electronic commerce) settings there are of course several similarities between the customers' situations. Both might be wondering how long the delivery will take, how to return the product, if the product is kept in stock, etc. Nevertheless, the example also illustrates important differences between the two situations depending on what type of product the customer wants to buy. In this case, it is obvious that the "skirt customer" has to find answers to more product related questions before ordering compared to the "CD customer". When a company offers its products on distance from the customers, the traditional face-to-face communication has to be replaced by other ways of communicating. The company has to decide through which communication media the customer interaction should be conducted. Such decisions might be made with several purposes; e.g., to be cost-effective and offer automated communication media, or to compete with a high degree of customer service and thus, offer many manually handled communication media that allow personal customer contact.

Several studies indicate that satisfied customers tend to become loyal to the company, which render long-term profitability. Providing customer service of high quality is even more important in distance selling than in physical business settings (face-to-face), according to (M Singh, 2008). In order to establish long-term customer relationships, companies have to communicate with their customers. For distance selling companies this means that they have to offer communication media that the customers appreciate, in order for them to become satisfied according to (Dabholkar, 2000). Before the

Internet era, customer communication in distance selling companies was mainly performed by telephone or mail. Nowadays, these companies have much more alternatives for their customer interaction, which implies more opportunities to establish long-term relationships. This new situation also means that the choices of communication media has become an important issue for distance selling companies. Therefore, it is critical to learn more about different communication media, both from a customer and a company perspective.

The researcher explores the importance of the product type and its implications for business-to-consumer (B2C) interaction in electronic commerce. As the example above shows, different types of products give rise to various customer questions, both before, during, and after an order is placed. This is important to consider when deciding which communication media to offer customers and which business actions that should be possible to perform through a certain medium. Unfortunate decisions concerning which communication media a company offers its customers, could result in mismatches between the company's and the customers' preferences. Such mismatches might obviously in the long run by threatening against the company's presence. The study confronts this problem by discussing product type as an important feature when choosing B2C communication media in electronic commerce settings.

2.2 TRENDS IN APPAREL AND LIFESTYLE SHOPPING

As reported by (Shweta, 2013) online apparel and lifestyle shopping is growing rapidly in India. This is highly likely because of the rising urbanization in the country. Small towns and cities are catching on strongly to the trends which were previously limited to the major metros not so many years ago. The easy accessibility of low cost smartphones and mobile Internet is getting these folks to explore online shopping in larger numbers. Besides this, there is evidence that this growing urbanization has resulted in people having more disposable cash. Another reason could be the growing fashion sensibilities in the country because of the increased connections between the metros and the other cities.

This makes apparel a hugely promising category when it comes to online shopping and the study indicates that there are now significant opportunities for growth in terms of sales for online fashion merchants.

Homeshop18 had analyzed the shopping trends in the country by looking into their customer base and found that clothing has the highest demand compared to other categories on their website, with one garment being sold every 40 seconds in the country. Sundeep Malhotra, the CEO of Homeshop18 also mentioned that customer centric features like Cash on Delivery and EMI are contributing significantly to this increase in apparel sales.

It seems now that most of the pioneering work done by early e-commerce companies like Flipkart, Infibeam, Myntra etc. has finally borne fruit because more Indians are getting used to the idea of online shopping, especially in a segment like apparel which was traditionally bought in retail stores. According to Ashutosh Lawania, co-founder of Myntra, the apparel segment looks like it will overtake electronics in the coming years.

Another interesting insight came from Deepa Thomas of eBay India who said that women in the country are becoming very savvy shoppers online and thus the drivers behind the clothing and lifestyle category's surge in sales. On eBay India, the apparel and lifestyle category accounts for 41% of the total transactions carried out. eBay noted that Kurtis ranks fifth amongst the top traded products in the category while Sarees ranked fourth amongst the top sold products.

2.3 TREMENDOUS ECONOMIC VALUE

According to a report by (IAMAI-IMRB, 2016) Ecommerce to touch Rs 2.1 trillion. The Digital Commerce Market has grown at a CAGR of 30%, between December 2011 and December 2015 and was valued at Rs 125,732 crores by the end of December 2015. It is estimated to reach Rs 211,005 crores by December 2016, according to the Digital Commerce Report 2015, published by the Internet and Mobile Association of India (IAMAI) and IMRB in June, 2016.

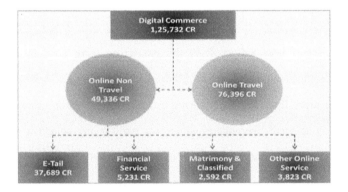

Figure 2.1 Digital commerce

Source: IAMAI-IMRB, June, 2016

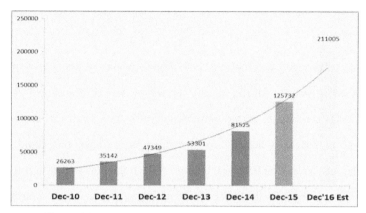

Figure 2.2 Growth of Ecommerce in India
Source: IAMAI-IMRB, June, 2016

The report finds that online travel industry continues to grow strongly with 61% share while share of online non-travel has improved over the previous year to reach 39%. In December 2015 share of e-Tail was 29%. Mobile Phone and Accessories, PCs and Apparel and Footwear continue to be the dominant categories that are selling within the e-tail segment. According to Nilotpal Chakravarti, AVP -IAMAI, "The growth trajectory of digital commerce signifies the coming of age of online transactions in India. No longer are Indians wary of transacting online. Another notable facet of the report is the substantial growth in non-travel online transactions."

Domestic air ticket and railways booking continue to be among top contributors to the Online Travel spends. These were the segments that were the top contributors in previous year also. Hotel Booking has seen a substantial growth at 165%, from Rs 1965 crores in December 2014 to Rs 5200 crores in December 2015. Online railway ticket booking has also grown at around 34%

from Rs 16200 crores in 2014 to Rs 21708 crores in 2015. Online travel was also expected to grow at a CAGR of around 40% to reach Rs 122815 crores by end of 2016.

The report also finds that E-Tailing maintained a strong performance with a 57% growth. Among E-Tail categories, Mobile Phone and Mobile Accessories continue to be the top contributor to the overall pie. Given that there is an increased demand for Smartphones in India, this could be a contributing factor. Computer and consumer electronics, as well as apparel and accessories, account for the bulk of India retail ecommerce spends contributing close to 49% collective to overall spend in E-Tail segment. Apparel and Footwear sale has almost doubled as compared to 2014, recording a 52% from Rs. 4699 crores in December 2014 to Rs 7142 crores in December 2015. This segment is expected to gain further momentum and reach Rs 72639 crores by end of 2016.

Component share of E Tail (Rs 37,689 CR)		
Mobile Phones + Mobile Accessories	14,109	37%
Apparels + Footwear + Personal / Healthcare Accessories	7,142	19%
Consumer Durables + Kitchen Appliances	6,452	17%
Laptops / Net books / Tablets / Desktops	4,726	13%
Home Furnishings	1,468	4%
Jewellery	1,120	3%
Other Products (Vouchers / Coupons, Toys, Gifts, Flowers, Handicrafts, Stationary etc.)	994	3%
Books	875	2%
Cameras + Camera Accessories	803	2%

Figure 2.3 Various Ecommerce business share in India
Source: IAMAI-IMRB, June, 2016

2.4 YOUNGER DEMOGRAPHIC

About 75% of online users are in the age group of 15-34 years since India is one of the youngest demography globally. "This is expected to be a continuing trend in coming years, given the age distribution in India", said D S Rawat, ASSOCHAM Secretary General. It is not surprising to see the growth among categories focused on younger audiences in the last 12 months.

According to (IAMAI, 2017), the maximum online shoppers are from the 15-24 years of age group, comprising both of males and females.

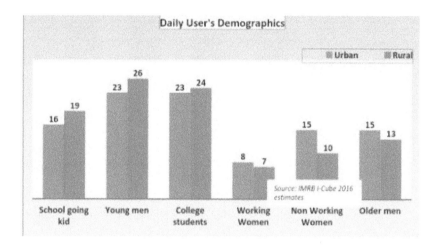

Figure 2.4 Male and Female Internet Users
Source IMRB I-Cube 2016 estimates

Overall, according to the report, young men and college going students are the primary users of the internet.

2.5 INTERNET USERS

A report titled 'Internet in India 2016' by the Internet and Mobile Association of India (IAMAI) jointly published by the IMRB, mentioned that the number of internet users in India is expected to reach between 450-465 million by June 2017. It adds that the country had 432 million mobile internet users in December 2016, of which 269 million, or 62.3% were from urban India and 163 million, or 37.7% were from rural India.

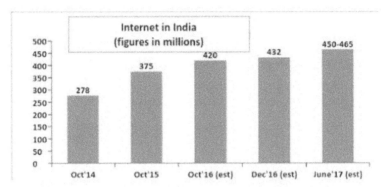

Figure : 2.5 Internet users in India

Source :   IMRB I-cube, All India Estimates December estimates does not account the impact of demonetization

According to the report, 51% of urban Internet users or 137.19 million use internet daily, while 90% of urban Internet users or 242 million use the internet at least once a month. On the other hand, in rural India, 78 million users or around 48% use the internet daily, while 140 million, or around 83% use the internet at least once a month.

According to a report by (Radhika, 2015) An unsettling revelation is the gender gap when it comes to access to Internet. Men account for 71 per cent of Internet users, while women account for just 29 per cent. The gap is slightly lower in urban India, with men accounting for 62 per cent and women 38 per cent. The gap is quite stark in rural India where the men to women Internet user ratio stand at 88:12.

The demographic data in the report also point to some interesting trends. In rural India, 75 per cent of the users fall in the 18–30 years age bracket, while 11 per cent are younger than 18 and 8 per cent are in the 31–45 years group. In Urban India, 32 per cent of monthly active users are college-going students.

Online communication, social networking, and entertainment are the top reasons for accessing the Internet. Only 24 per cent of urban users and 5 per cent of rural users accessed the Internet for online shopping.

2.6 RISE OF MOBILE COMMERCE

It has been observed that mobile commerce (m-commerce) is growing rapidly as a stable and secure supplement to the ecommerce industry due to aggressive online discounts, rising fuel price and wider and abundant choices. Shopping online through smart phones is proving to be a game changer, and industry leaders believe that m-commerce could contribute up to 70 per cent of their total revenues.

According to (Satinder, 2015) "The Impact Of Mobile Commerce In India: A Swot Analysis", India is the largest mobile market in the world after china. The number of internet users in India reached 302 million in December, 2014 according to a survey of IAMAI and IMRB international. 2014 has been a landmark year for India in the sector of M-commerce. According to Nielsen survey in 2014, smartphone penetration in Indonesia was (23%), India (18%) and the Philippines (15%). In India, Wi-Fi is often used by mobile users in shopping malls or internet cafes. There are 3G and 4G connections in India.

According to PayPal mobile commerce, the transaction made with mobile phones increased in 2014 by over 250% compare with the year 2013. Smartphones and "Mobile Only" Internet users are growing rapidly in India.

According to a report by (Radhika, 2015) It is not surprising anymore that mobile is responsible for a big chunk of the growth of Internet. In Urban India, the mobile Internet user base grew by 65 per cent as compared to 2014 to reach 197 million in October 2015. In Rural India, the mobile Internet user base was expected to reach 87 million by December 2015 and 109 million by June 2016.

Ninety-four per cent of users access the Internet through their mobile phones in Urban India. However, 64 per cent also use the desktop or laptop to access the Internet. But 90 per cent of those who use the mobile to access the Internet consider it their primary device for browsing.

2.7 ECOMMERCE MARKET IN INDIA

According to Assocham study India's e-commerce market was worth about $3.8 billion (roughly Rs. 25,692 crores) in 2009, it went up to $17 billion (roughly Rs. 1,14,940 crores) in 2014 and to $23 billion (roughly Rs. 1,55,507 crores) in 2015 and was expected to touch a whopping $38 billion-mark (roughly Rs. 2,56,925 crores) by 2016.

2.8 BLENDING VIDEO AND ECOMMERCE

(Siwicki, 2006) suggested blending video and e-commerce. Some retailers are capitalizing on the explosive growth of online video, seeking to better showcase products and entertain and engage customers. Weaving online video into ecommerce sites to enhance the customer web experience is where the action's at.

The aim is to better inform shoppers about products in a way that text, Imagery and audio cannot, and/or to entertain shoppers in a manner that increases brand awareness and turns shoppers into customers. Online video is the latest technology to further advance the Internet.

Out of endless number of e-commerce sites storming the ecommerce business world, the top 10 best sites in India according to (techinasia May 30 , 2016) for apparels which were studied are as follows:

1. Ebay.in

Ebay.in has become one of the major online shopping sites which feature high end products of good quality at a reasonable price. Whether you are looking for old or new products, you can find them all in this one place that holds its position strongly in the online marketing biggies. Boasting of a wide array of products from renowned brands, this online portal has won the hearts of the customers with its professional services.

Features:

- Convenient
- Consistent
- Affordable
- Great professional support

2. India times shopping

The Times of India group brings the India times shopping website that is considered as one of the oldest e-commerce platform that has been doing well since the beginning. With a diverse range of categories such as apparels, footwear, sunglasses, bags, kitchen, electronics, home decor, computers, health and beauty, etc., the online store has been offering an enjoyable shopping experience to each and every customer.

Features:

- Hassle-free shopping experience
- Low prices
- Huge collection
- Fast delivery

3. Askmebazaar

At Askmebazaar you will be enthralled to find the wide range of products available at a great value price along with impeccable offers and deals. Be it a local brand or an Indian brand, each and every product you ask for will live up to your expectations. Though it is new member in the world of ecommerce, it has a rich collection of products and offer all with good discounts that helps customers to save a good amount on their purchase.

Features:

- Simple and easy to use
- Trustworthy products
- Satisfying user experience
- Quicker delivery

4. Shop clues

The latest entry to the world of e-commerce hub is Shop clues that has very efficiently marked its position in a very short period of time. It is focusing mainly on the daily household needs, mobiles phones and electronics and is striving to rise up the ladders in the near future. It is garnering very good name and fame owing to the good quality products offered in the most competitive market price.

Features:

- Varied range of payment methods
- Good quality products
- Highly affordable
- Easy and fast delivery

5. Myntra

Myntra, a Bangalore based company is swiping off the market demands of the young generation by bringing forward to them sophisticated yet elegant fashion and lifestyle products. It has tie-ups with the most renowned fashion brands that ensure a perfect platform for each and every fashion shoppers. So, whether you want to buy a casual dress for a day out or a glittery shoe for a party, Myntra has got them all for all types of occasions.

Features:

- Hassle-free experience
- Convenient
- Easy return policy
- Excellent support team

6. Amazon.in

This highly renowned and trusted US e-commerce company spread its dimensions to India in the year 2013 and showered the website with an extensive range of amazing products and offers for the Indian audience. From fashion to electronic items, from accessories to beauty care products, from furniture to home decor items, look out for anything at Amazon, you will surely be astonished to see the variety of options that it provides.

Features:

- Fast and reliable
- Trustworthy quality products
- Excellent customer support
- Safe and fast shipping

7. <u>Paytm</u>

Launched in the year 2010, this Indian e-commerce site started off with just online mobile, electricity bills and DTH recharge facility. But after 4 years, it launched the paytm wallet which became an unstoppable craze amongst the audience. Right now this electronic wallet has more than 40 million accounts making life of every individual simpler with the biggest electronic wallet facility.

Features:

- Exclusive cash backs
- Hassle-free payment
- Quick in delivery
- Easy refundable

8. Snap deal

Yet another well-liked e-commerce site that has rose to great fame and admiration is the 2010 established company is Snap deal. Featuring high quality products in top class categories such as mobiles, books, electronic items, apparels, etc., snap deal is sticking strong to its tagline, 'Dil ki Deal'. It has garnered huge name and fame for itself owing to its impeccable products and high level of authenticity.

Features:

- Reliable quality products
- Renowned brands
- Highly popular
- Good delivery service

9. Jabong

Jabong is considered as one of the top fashion portal that offers a wide array of 90,000 plus products, 2, 00,000 plus styles and more than 2,000 high-end brands, both national and international. Be it fashion clothing, trendy accessories or pretty home décor, it is highly admired amongst the youth. The products are not only trendy and belong to best brands, but are available in pocket-friendly rate.

Features:

- User-friendly and convenient
- Affordable products
- Reliable and trustworthy
- Easy payment options

10. Flipkart

The site that tops the list of best e-commerce site is none other than the extravagantly popular Flipkart. Co-founded by Sachin Bansal and Binny Bansal right back in the year 2007, the company has only soar to great heights. While it was an online book store before, it later added on several other categories such as electronic items, apparels, gadgets and much more. When you are looking out for trust and security, Flipkart does stand on the specified grounds strongly.

Features:

- Reliable service
- Easy navigation
- Easy refund process
- Professional help support

2.9 STUDY ON RETURNS

According to (Kim, 2005), "Factors influencing consumers' apparel purchasing intention in the C2C ecommerce market", India's online fashion market is set for a boom period, because of a young demographic and strong economic growth, so it is essential that ecommerce companies and their designers know what is going to appeal to the market.

Increasing internet penetration, increased smartphone usage and growing preference for online shopping will help online fashion players grab a sizeable chunk of India's organized retail sector that would touch $180 billion by the year 2020. The Indian fashion sector is currently dominated by apparel, followed by accessories, footwear and finally lingerie.

According to the analytics research, ethnic clothing is not just the highest apparel catalog item in terms of density, but also has the highest average selling price (Rs 2,055) and discount rate (average: Rs 1,816) - proof that ethnic is very desirable for the Indian consumer.

An overwhelming 69 per cent of the entire national apparel catalog is targeted towards female customers, with men's wear at 21 per cent and children at 9 per cent. So there are still some real opportunities to be had with these gaps in the marketplace.

Accessories are the big ticket Women can never have too many handbags or jewels, and this appears to be true when it comes to online shopping. Jewelry is the highest selling sector and also covets the highest average selling price per item (Rs 6,552) per item, with, again, the highest average discount (Rs 2,547). Watches come in second, followed by bags/handbags, with average prices of Rs 2,891 and 1,587 respectively.

According to the researcher and the analysis of average Indian consumer online, shopping for fashion, highlights the fact that Omni-channel retailing is the way forward. Retailers who see digital as an integral part of their business will thrive in fashion, while 'big data analytics' clearly has the power to integrate brick and mortar with digital.

According to (Klas, 2013) in his research "On Aligning Returns Management with the Ecommerce Strategy to Increase Effectiveness", returns can be categorized into two groups: controllable and uncontrollable. In essence, the controllable can be eliminated before they occur and the cause or causes can be minimized or avoided through actions taken in the supply chain (Stock et al., 2006). Conversely, the uncontrollable returns are unavoidable in the short term.

Consumer returns are perhaps the most difficult as they are unpredictable and therefore difficult to anticipate, which affects the handling and execution of the return. From a B2C perspective, consumer returns are naturally the main returns flow and should be differentiated by the cause of return. If the cause of return is not a consumer error, the best procedure might be to target reconciliation with the consumer and thereby reduce the harm caused... However, Ferguson et al. (2006) argue that consumer product returns are driven by a "consumer is king" attitude supported by liberal product returns policies. "Not all consumer returns are a token of a bad sale or a dissatisfied consumer; some organizations are even managing product returns policies to maximize their future profits" according to Rosenbaum et al. (2003) and Petersen et al. (2010). From a company perspective, despite the cost of returns, i.e. handling and refunding, the customers' ability to return may have a positive impact on future purchases and long-term profits (Petersen, 2010).

In e-commerce, consumer returns are an inherent element of shopping online due to the customer's inability to experience a particular product and/or service prior to ordering. However, the returns policy and its leniency might also result in consumer abuse Kang et al. (2009) and research has found that nearly 20% of consumers engage in some type of "illegitimate product returns" Piron et al. (2003).

The researcher has also mentioned that besides all the advantages of online buying which includes 24/7 availability, lower price and convenience, the internet as an intermediary creates a distance between the buyer and the sellers. This physical distance is evident in certain products in which consumers struggle to evaluate product and services before ordering, thus certain consumers might hesitate to use ecommerce and do not purchase clothes online. They always want to see or try clothes on first before they shop online. Return policy gives organization an opportunity to differentiate themselves from their competitors and to attract hesitant non-adopters.

According to series of paper discussing ecommerce, (Amrish, 2011) General Manager, First Data India and ICICI Merchant Services, a report on "E-commerce: A Boon for the Current Economic Downturn in the year 2011. Which says that by the end of 2011, the ecommerce market in India had clocked close to Rs 50,000 cores? In the year 2012, even though there were less than 10 million internet users who were actually engaging in e-commerce activities, there were about 150 million internet users in India or around 75 million households that were ready for e-commerce (Internet & Mobile Association of India). The growing reach in terms of internet connectivity to the interiors of India coupled with the positive experiences of end consumers when buying online beyond the metros and big cities were the key drivers of the e-commerce boon in India. Businesses in even the smallest towns and villages were becoming increasingly aware of e-commerce and were excited by the growth potential.

In 2012, consumers across urban India were confident enough to make purchases that exceeded Rs 20,000-25,000. Earlier, the same shoppers stayed in the Rs 2,000-5,000 ranges. According to a study (Vizisense –report on e-commerce) almost 57% of business for e-commerce product sites came from tier I, tier II and tier III cities while the eight metros accounted for the remainder 43%. The same pattern was visible in the service sites too, with tier I, tier II and tier III cities contributing 54% of revenue versus 46 % by the eight metros. Seeing the immense growth e-commerce can offer, merchants across the country were increasingly keen to find out how their businesses can capitalize on the online business model. E-commerce facilitates shopping anytime, anywhere and for almost anything desired. Busy consumers prefer this to the restrictions of when a mall/shop is open and the need to physically travel to a shop. Online business takes shopping a step further by taking itself to the customer creating conveniences of shopping anywhere and at any time.

The key reasons for the success of e-commerce, success are summarized below.

- Shopping 24x7:

E-commerce facilitates shopping anytime, anywhere and for almost anything desired. Busy consumers prefer this to the restrictions of when a mall/shop is open and the need to physically travel to a shop. Online business takes shopping a step further by taking itself to the customer creating conveniences of shopping anywhere and at any time.

- Reduced operational cost:

Since the entire business can be moved online, the need for physical stores has become obsolete. Less infrastructural investment and associated labor costs drives up the profit margin. The seller can then transfer this benefit to the customer in the form of discounted pricing which boosts the appeal of online shopping. Easy to compare:

It is far easier and quicker to compare prices of goods online, equipping the customer with the information to decide the right price or terms for themselves. The comparison is not restricted to items from a single seller, or a single region. One can explore products across global markets via e-commerce.

- Safe & secure:

Customers can trust the process of going online and purchasing only when transactions are fast, convenient and secure. A high degree of integrity is possible only when the online electronic payment provider is reputable and trustworthy. In India, all payment transaction providers are required to comply with the security requirements laid out by the Reserve Bank of India making the system more robust and reliable. Increased reach for the merchant: Just as the customer finds them able to venture across geographic markets, the merchant too is able to display his product to customers in new territories. Market penetration also becomes far more achievable with e-commerce; it is possible for a merchant in Mumbai to extend his reach to north-eastern cities or even rural villages that are now connected by the online network.

- Social media trend:

In India, with the increasing propensity of social media, businesses have now begun to engage their customers on social networking portals such as Facebook. Promotions, sales and new products are increasingly showcased through such channels and mobile apps are now available that suggest products to users based on their profiles. These are likely to be rapidly developing marketing channels for the future. The e-commerce world is changing rapidly in the digitized world. These e-commerce developments may have been accelerated by the global economic downturn which may be driving consumers to find new ways of reducing their costs of living. The online channel offers a clear value proposition for both merchants and consumers making it the most sought after and exciting business model today.

According to Lantz et al. (2013) "Real e-customer behavioural responses to free delivery and free returns", besides the upsides of online sales, such as availability 24/7, an increased product range, lower price and convenience, there are some downsides to online shopping as well. The

Internet as an intermediary in itself creates a distance between the buyer (in this case the consumer) and the seller's (in this case the e-tailer's) products. This physical distance is evident in certain businesses in which consumers struggle to evaluate products and services before ordering, thus certain consumers might hesitate to use the e-commerce distribution channel. The expected value of a potential customer is lower when returns are free. According to the researcher following assumptions were made:

- Free returns increase the probability of return from 16 % to 20 %.
- The average value of returned items is not significantly affected by free returns.
- The return fee for customers is 39 SEK
- Free returns increase the probability of orders from 24 % to 26 %.
- The number of orders per unique customer is not significantly affected by free returns.
- Free returns decrease the average value of orders from 744 SEK to 712 SEK.
- The average contribution margin ratio is about 2/3.

Clothing goods are non-digital products due to their performance only being able to be evaluated in the post-purchase stage. Clothing can further be broken down to extrinsic and intrinsic criteria. Extrinsic criteria refer to rather factual information i.e. price or brand Reimer et al. (2005), whereas "intrinsic product attributes are those that cannot be changed without altering the physical characteristics of the product", according to Yeung et al. (2004). According to Golletz et al. (2010) who consequently studied apparel return criteria it becomes obvious that dissatisfaction with intrinsic apparel criteria predominantly leads to product returns and therefore needs the most attention in virtual surroundings. Clothing return criteria by Park et al. (2002) find size, color and fit most important product-decision criteria. (Beck, 2000) defines "poor fit, bad drape, or unpleasant feel while wearing the item, or surprise as to the color of the garment" to be return reasons. Jacobs et al. (2007) stated that, "unknown quality of products, fitting, size, and originality of apparel can all be additional risks implied by the type of product category purchased via the Internet." Ill-fitting garments, the main reason to return garments. Other reason were Long delivery process, Wrong product delivered, Material or product defect, Product did not fulfill expectations, Wrong fit, Wrong size, Different silhouette, Different colors and Different material criteria.

According to Bohdanowicz et al. (1994) the purchase-decision process is generally composed of three phases, namely: pre-purchase, purchase and post-purchase phase. 1 information search– 2 product selection– 3 purchase evaluation– 4 purchase decision.– 1 information search– 2 product selection– 3 purchase hesitance– 4 purchase decision– 5 purchase evaluation (Online) In order to make the virtual purchase process more efficient, thus to decrease perceived risk prior to purchase and avoid product returns post purchase, the actual physical product evaluation must be moved forward within the apparel purchase process. This is due to the fact that– in apparel– the process step 'fitting' occurs post buying instead of the other way around. When expressing this process in a more abstract manner, it can be summarized as 'surfing, buying and fitting'. The product evaluation occurs post buying as well and is thus more likely to turn out negatively. The purchase-decision-making step must be aligned with the post-purchase-evaluation step to decrease product risk and dissatisfaction consequently. The process of 'surf, buy and fit' must thus ideally be transformed into 'surfing, fitting and then buying'. When moving the evaluation part– based on the fitting of the product– further up the process, one can shorten the entire supply chain, therewith fundamentally optimizing it. Non-digital products require special attention when marketed online. "Many of the characteristics of a garment that are pivotal to the consumer decision-making process– color, feel, and fit– are difficult, if not impossible, to communicate virtually", conclude (Hammond and Kohler, 2002). (Jacobs and de Klerk, 2007) define what has been found by others as well.

"The inability to assess and evaluate apparel items physically through the Internet is therefore one of the more significant risks that consumers may experience in terms of online apparel purchasing." (Goldsmith and Goldsmith, 2002) consider online apparel sales to be a huge challenge. Traditionally, apparel consumers assess and or evaluate their potential purchases offline because it requires touch, feel and fit. Park et al. (2005); Jacobs et al. (2007). It is essential to challenge this exact problem by revising the process. They concluded that, the more elaborate the purchase process, the more elaborate the decision making and the more likely the possibility to perceive risk. It can herewith be concluded that non-digital goods such as apparel, require an adjusted purchase process that moves product evaluation further up within the supply chain. By allowing the consumer to physically evaluate the product prior to the actual online purchase, major risk concerns could be diminished. In case of apparel, the most important information is intrinsic and further narrowed down to fit and size.

2.10 REASONS FOR RETURNS

Jan Hammond et al. (2000) reviewed that the difficulty in characterizing the product is the personal, often emotional nature of an apparel purchase. Apparel purchasing decisions are closely linked to individuals' feelings about themselves, their body image, and the image they wish to project. Clothing is the "skin" a person chooses to wear to project his or her self-image to the public, and hence is intimately tied to one's sense of self. Thus the decision can be laden with emotional factors that are less important in decisions to buy books, music, food, and electronics.

The accuracy of color on the web is of particular concern to consumers. A web based survey conducted by Info Trends Research Group, Inc. indicated that 88% of consumers would prefer to shop at an internet site that could guarantee "true and accurate" color. However, the respondents indicated that they rarely purchase apparel on-line, "largely because of their insecurity about getting what they expect."

The report indicated that many consumers who purchase apparel online refer to printed catalogs for more accurate depictions of color. The degree to which the difficulty in characterizing apparel products inhibits online consumer purchases differs by product type.

Basic products are selling well on-line, according to Forrester research "Apparel's On-line Makeover,". These products have a number of characteristics that make them more amenable to on-line purchasing. First, they are fairly familiar products, making their descriptions easier to understand. The touch and feel of basic garments are quite familiar and are fairly similar across brands, which makes the buyer less hesitant to purchase them "sight unseen," and produces fewer surprises when the garment arrives.

Similarly, for more basic items, the fit of different garment styles tends to be better understood, making it easier to purchase online. In some cases, the cut of a basic garment may be more forgiving in that it can fit a wide range of body types. Products like men's dress shirts and women's hosiery with consistent, known sizing are also amenable to on-line buying. Basic garments are typically lower cost than more fashionable products, which also contributes to a lower level of risk in an on-line purchase. In addition, since basic products are worn for "everyday" events, their purchase often evokes less emotion than more fashion-forward items.

More fashionable items may be more risky to purchase on line: the decision to purchase online is more significant because of the increased importance of touch and feel, color and cost, and the increased emotional element associated with more fashionable clothing. However, the internet is expected to penetrate the fashion segments of the market, in part because it will provide exposure and access to unique or unusual products that are hard for consumers to find locally. The ability to customize clothing for fit, fabric, or style should also provide an impetus to increase on-line sales of fashionable garments. Several initiatives are underway to improve the ability of on-line sites to characterize their products, and thereby reduce both the hesitancy of consumers to purchase apparel.

According to Arun Thamizhvanan et al. (2013) in his study about "Determinants of customers' online purchase intention: an empirical study in India", he has mentioned that according to Associated Chambers of Commerce and Industry of India (ASSOCHAM), the size of the Indian online retail industry was INR 2000 crore in the year 2013 and the industry was projected a steady annual growth rate of 35 per cent to reach INR 7000 crore by 2015. Given the growing importance of the online retail industry in

India, it remained imperative for web retailers and internet marketers to understand the determinants of online customers' purchase intention to decipher what is important to the Indian online customer. According to the author, the determinants of online purchase intention among youth in the Indian context were as follows:

- Males were found to have more intention to shop online than females.
- The internet savvy students contributed the major share of online buyers.
- Indian online shoppers typically tend to seek offers and great value price deals instead of brand or quality. Online retailers may target the impulse purchase orientation nature of Indian consumers and should be focusing on increasing online trust.

According to study conducted by Lee Mi Yeon et al.(2013) the satisfaction levels and preferences of consumer's purchase experience and the sizing system showed that 48.6% of the total respondents were dissatisfied with the current sizing system and it was suggested that by establishing globally compatible sizing system, consumers would be able to recognize their sizes on their own and by doing this, it will lower perceived risk of the consumers at the time of an Internet shopping mall purchase, and this will raise their level of satisfaction while making purchases.

According to a study conducted by (Subhash Masanappa Suryawanshi, 2017) in the area of "E- Commerce in India - Challenges and Opportunities", E-Commerce industry is growing at an astounding rate in India and is expected to account for 1.61% of the global GDP by 2018. According to a report by Forrester, India is set to become the fastest growing market in the Asia-Pacific region with an expected growth rate of over 57% between 2012 and 2016. According to the researcher, recent trends in Indian e-commerce industry were as follows:

1) Men in India shop three times more than women while women continue to dominate the in-store markets, men with disposable incomes have taken it upon themselves to play the larger role in online shopping.

2) Cash-On-Delivery (COD) remains the most preferred online payment method. Indians love the Cash-On-Delivery option; it gives them more control over online transactions since they don't have to pay until the product is at their doorstep. COD option during checkout has also been proven to boost impulse purchases.

3) 60% of online purchases happen during business hours (9AM-5PM). This proven trend is a myth-buster that shows how integral a part online shopping has become in day-to-day lives. Marketers can use this fact to schedule their promotions across advertising channels accordingly.

4) The Rural Pitch Ecommerce companies emphasize more on attracting the customers from rural areas. Along with this, traditional business houses such as Tata Group and Reliance Industries will enter more aggressively into the ecommerce business.

5) Smartphone Apps: However, users browse products on desktops or laptops, they prefer transacting via smart phones because of their faster linkages to payment gateways. Smartphone ecommerce apps are also preferred as they offer more personalized shopping experience for customers and a better understanding of consumers for the ecommerce company.

Indian e-commerce has seen impressive growth in the last few years. Considering India's demographic dividend and rising internet accessibility, the sector is slated to scale greater heights. Rising standards of living, availability of wider product ranges, reduced prices and busy lifestyles reveal this fact more prominently thereby giving way to online deals on gift vouchers. Going by the statistics, e-commerce market in India is expected to nearly double to Rs.2, 11,005crores by December according to industry body Internet and Mobile Association of India (IAMAI). The market grew 30% between December 2011 and December 2015.

The rapidly increasing 3G internet users and a recent introduction of 4G across the country has played an important role in the growth. Explosive growth of Smartphone users. Rising standards of living as result of fast decline in poverty rate. Availability of much wider product range. Competitive prices compared attractive to the customers. Increased usage of online classified sites, with more consumers buying and selling second-hand goods.

There are some barriers responsible for slow growth of e-commerce in India. Some barrier in using e-commerce including security problems,

1. In India, Cash on delivery is the preferred payment mode: In India, most of the people prefer to pay cash on delivery due to the low credit card diffusion and low trust in online transactions. Not like electronic payments, manual cash collection is quite perilous, expensive and laborious.

2. Infrastructural Problems: Internet is the backbone of e-commerce. Internet penetration in India is still very low (34.8%) compared to other countries. The quality of connectivity is poor in several regions. But both these are real threats for the growth e-commerce market in India

3. Incorrect postal address: When the customer places an online order, he will get a call from the company, asking about his exact location. The given address is not enough because there is always a little standardization while writing post addresses. It is also one of the biggest challenges that faced by e-commerce in India.

4. Absence of Cyber Laws: Other big challenge associated with e-commerce market is the near absence of cyber laws to regulate transactions on the Net. WTO is expected to enact cyber laws soon. The India's Information Technology (IT) Bill passed by the Indian Parliament on May 17, 2000 intends to tackle legislatively the growing areas in e-commerce. As it stand today, the Bill deals with only commercial and criminal areas of law. However, it does not take care of issues such as individual property rights, content regulation to privacy and data protection specific legislation.

5. Privacy and Security Concern: In case of startup and small business, Business owners fail to take the initial steps to secure and protect their online business through installation of authentic protection services like antivirus and firewall protection, which indeed a crucial step for successful online business players. Usage of unauthorized soft wares will not protect the customer.

6. Payment and Tax Related Issues: Tax rate system of Indian market is another factor for lesser growth rate of e-commerce in India in comparison to other developed countries like USA and UK. In those countries, tax rate is uniform for all sectors whereas tax structure of India varies from sector to sector. This factor creates accounting problems for the Indian online business companies. The Government of India is committed to replace all the indirect taxes levied on goods and services by the Centre and States and

implement Goods and Services Tax (GST) by April 2017.One-Country-One-Tax is the main motive of GST.

7. Touch and Feel' factors: Indian customers are more comfortable in buying products physically. They tend to choose the product by touching the product directly. Thereby, Indian buyers are more inclined to do ticketing and booking online in Travel sectors, books and electronics. Companies dealing with products like apparel, handicrafts, jewelry have to face challenges to sell their products as the buyers want to see and touch before they buy these stuffs.

8. Shipping Challenges: Issues related to lack of supply chain integration, high delivery charges for products, delay in delivery and lack of proper courier services in some areas also make customers frustrated.

9. Product Return, Refund etc. Product which is not satisfactory for the customers tends to get replaced or returned. This is another major issue which leads into overall loss in revenue, loss of shipment costs and more than all these loss of your reputation.

10. Customer Service: E- Marketers focuses on the website performance ignoring customer relationship and in-personal assistance.

2.11 SUMMARY

Literature survey can be summarized as follows:

a. In India there are about 75% of online users in the age group of 15-34 years. . In rural India, 75 per cent of the users fall in the 18–30 years age bracket, while 11 per cent are younger than 18 and 8 per cent are in the 31–45 years group. In Urban India, 32 per cent of monthly active users are college-going students.), the number of internet users in India is expected to reach between 450-465 million by June 2017 (ASSOCHAM and IMRB).

b. According to Ashutosh Lawania, co-founder of Myntra, the apparel segment looks like it will overtake electronics in the coming years.

c. Another interesting insight came from Deepa Thomas of eBay India who said that women in the country are becoming very savvy shoppers online and thus the drivers behind the clothing and lifestyle category's surge in sales. On eBay India, the apparel and lifestyle category accounts for 41% of the total transactions carried out. eBay noted that Kurtis ranks fifth amongst the top traded products in the category while Sarees ranked fourth amongst the top sold products.

d. According to Jan Hammond et al. (2000) A web based survey conducted by Info Trends Research Group, Inc. indicated that 88% of consumers would prefer to shop at an internet site that could guarantee "true and accurate" color. However, the respondents indicated that they rarely purchase apparel on-line, "largely because of their insecurity about getting what they expect."

e. According to a study conducted by (Subhash Masanappa Suryawanshi, 2017) Touch and Feel' factors: Indian customers are more comfortable in buying products physically. They tend to choose the product by touching the product directly. Thereby,

Indian buyers are more inclined to do ticketing and booking online in Travel sectors, books and electronics

f. According to Lee Mi Yeon et al.(2013) the satisfaction levels and preferences of consumer's purchase experience and the sizing system showed that 48.6% of the total respondents were dissatisfied with the current sizing system

g. "Many of the characteristics of a garment that are pivotal to the consumer decision-making process– color, feel, and fit– are difficult, if not impossible, to communicate virtually", conclude (Hammond and Kohler, 2002). (Jacobs and de Klerk, 2007)

h. According to Bohdanowicz et al. (1994). The purchase-decision-making step must be aligned with the post-purchase-evaluation step to decrease product risk and dissatisfaction consequently.

i. According to Park et al. (2002) find size, color and fit most important product-decision criteria. (Beck, 2000) defines "poor fit, bad drape, or unpleasant feel while wearing the item, or surprise as to the color of the garment" to be return reasons. Jacobs et al. (2007) stated that, "unknown quality of products, fitting, size, and originality of apparel can all be additional risks implied by the type of product category purchased via the Internet."

j. According to Lantz, 2013 Free returns increase the probability of return from 16 % to 20 %.

CHAPTER 3

METHODOLOGY

3.1 INTRODUCTION

The main purpose of this research was to gather information about how consumers interact with the online buying environment of garments and more specifically the effect of that interaction and their experience. The two major approaches towards gathering of data about this research were primary and secondary research. The primary and secondary data is a congregation of data collected between 2013 and 2017 from online and offline customers, Industry experts and various other pioneers in the field.

The secondary research was done to understand the structure and dynamics of the electronic commerce marketplace in India. Information from various published resources like articles, books and journals were examined. The research required extensive reviewing of recent newspaper articles, white papers, corporate reports and blogs to perform a data validation check. This was due to lot of innovation happening around the world in the field of electronic commerce. The scope of the research was then defined within the geographical location of Bengaluru and age group targeted were millennials

The methodology can be summarized through the following diagram.

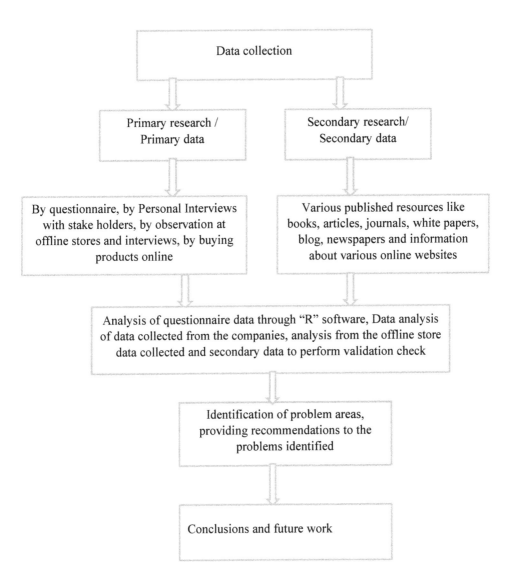

Figure 3.1 Methodology

3.2 PRIMARY RESEARCH

The primary research has been done using discrete data sources such as the following :

- Comprehensive study at the best apparel e-commerce company in Bengaluru
- By a questionnaire filled by customers who have purchased apparel online
- By conducting in-depth structured interviews with stakeholders of e-commerce industry in Bengaluru
- By data collected by observation at various offline stores.

3.2.1 Primary Data

3.2.1.1 Data collected from study at e-commerce Industry

A study was done with Flipkart, one of the leading e-commerce companies. The data for three months: December 2014, January 2015 and February 2015 was collected and compiled. The problem areas in online apparel businesses were considered and analysed.

3.2.1.2 Data collected through questionnaire

The data collected from Flipkart was used to work with the data sample for the questionnaire. The data size was formed using the following steps:

Step-1

Total number of buyers in three months:	6, 55,688
Sample size: 5% of population:	5/100 x 6, 55,688
Total:	32,784

Step-2

Cluster sampling was done based on dividing the sample population into a group (based upon geographical proximity such as Bengaluru), called City Cluster that has a correlation with the main variable online shopping

Research Method: Cluster sampling (geographical area)

Geographical area: Bengaluru = 15/100 x 32,784
15%:

Total: 4,917

Step-3

Selected element in the cluster (age group 18 to 30 years), using the SRS technique.

Element in cluster: Cluster (Age 18 – 30 years)

Age: (Millennials 18-30 years): 40% of 4,917

Total: 1,967

Step-4

Simple Random Sampling (SRS Technique): Out of 1,967 customers a random sampling was done. A questionnaire was filled by the buyers via e-mail and in person by 1000 respondents. The final data sample size was 891.

A questionnaire was formulated keeping in mind the following issues:

- Why do people shop for apparel online?
- Why do people prefer to buy apparel online over offline?
- What are the main reasons for returns?
- How can e-commerce apparel shopping experience be improved by use of technology?

3.2.1.3 Interviews with Industry Experts

In-depth interviews were conducted with numerous stakeholders of the e-commerce industry in Bengaluru including various leading companies viz. Myntra, Flipkart, Jabong, ABOF and Charmboard.

3.2.1.4 Data collected by study at offline stores

A study was done by observation at various trial rooms across several brick and mortar stores to understand the problem of size and fit. A data size of 100 was collected by personal interviews and through observation in order to understand the problem of size and fit in an offline store.

3.2.1.5 Data collected by Studying and experiencing various online stores

The forty best National and International e-commerce companies were studied. Several garments were purchased to understand the buying process and the problems associated from consumer perspective.

3.3 SECONDARY RESEARCH

Secondary research was done to understand the structure and dynamics of digital commerce marketplace in India. A data validation check was performed from information retrieved from various e-commerce companies

3.3.1 Secondary Data

1. Reviewed the current practices in e-commerce industry through published literature.

2. Reviewed various articles published by various researchers in the area of online apparel businesses published in various National and International Journals.

3.3.1.1 Studied and data collected for various websites

The most popular websites were studied. Distinct features in terms of customer offers, options available, size chart, fit solutions, return policies, views of the product, visual merchandising, colour choices and display were studied for the following websites:

Amazon, Flipkart, Fashionandyou, Snap Deal, Myntra, Dealsandyou, HomeShop18, Yebhi.com, ShopClues, Jabong, Limeroad, Koovs, Shoppers Stop and Voylla Retail.

This is what formed the data base for the primary research and secondary research.

CHAPTER 4

DATA ANALYSIS

4.1 INTRODUCTION

Data that was gathered from primary and secondary research has been thoroughly analysed in this chapter.

4.2 ANALYSIS OF DATA COLLECTED THROUGH QUESTIONNAIRE

Based on the study at Flipkart, the data size was formed as 1000. The data was collected via a questionnaire filled by 1000 customers who buy apparel online. The geographical proximity was Bangalore and the selected age group was 18-35years. The final data size was 891. The analysis has been done using "R" software. The following correlation were done to find the odds ratio to compare the impact of various attributes with respect to online shopping.

- The correlation between the attributes and their impact where people shifted from online buying to offline buying in the last six months.
- The correlation between the attributes and their impact where people shifted from offline to online shopping of apparel.
- The correlation between the attributes and their impact on people, who shop online.

The analysis is as follows:

a. The questionnaire was filled by online customers in the age group of 18 to 30 years. The number of male and female in each age group is as shown in table 4.1.

Table 4.1 Male and female in each age category

Age group	Female	Male	Grand Total
18-22 Years	216	183	399
23-26 Years	129	195	324
27-30 Years	48	120	168
Grand Total	**393**	**498**	**891**

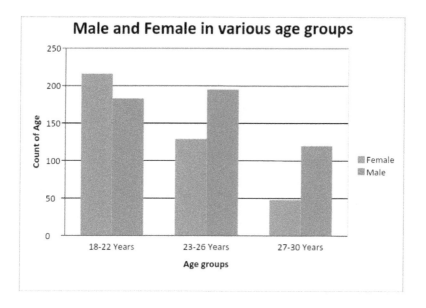

Figure 4.1 Male and female in various age groups

b. The reasons for shopping clothes from a physical store are shown in figure 4.2. 17% of customers prefer to shop from a physical store mainly because of its visual merchandising, 24% customers like to test for size and fit. They also like to touch and feel the fabric as seen in results indicated by 22% of the total. The ability to take the product home instantly at the is preferred by 20% and 17% of the customers are attracted by facility of speaking to the store manager as shown in figure 4.2.

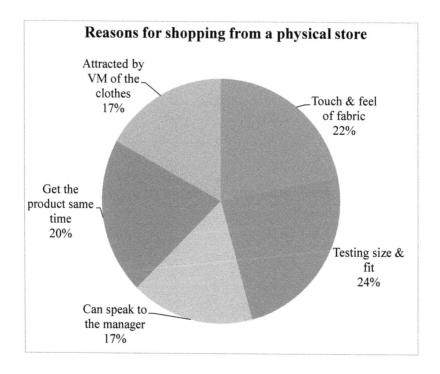

Figure 4.2 Reasons for shopping from a physical store

c. Online shopping is preferred by more than 17% of the government / private service individuals and a little above 15% of the students; however 14% of government individuals shop from physical stores and nearly 16.5% students prefer to shop from a physical store as shown in figure 4.3.

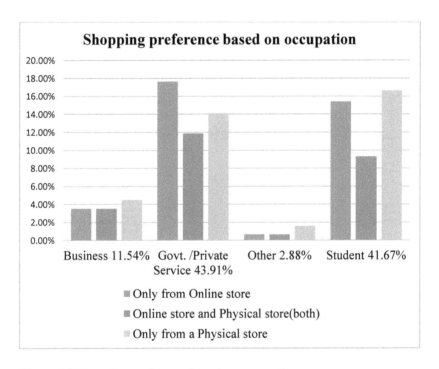

Figure 4.3 Shopping preference based on occupation

c. When do people prefer to buy clothes online?

It can be clearly seen from the analysis that 64% of customers prefer to buy clothes online due to all time discounts and lesser prices of garments as compared to the traditional way of shopping. This is followed by 15% of the people preferring to buy clothes offline due to unavailability of the garment offline. 12% of the customers prefer online shopping in the festival time whereas 9 % customers prefer to send gifts outstation. The analysis is shown in figure 4.4.

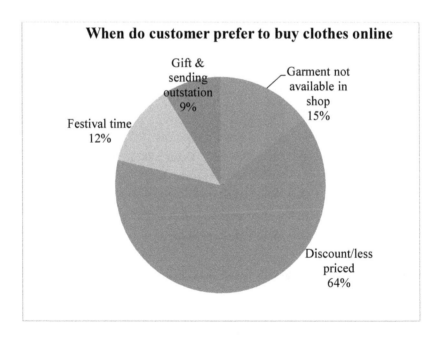

Figure 4.4 Customers preference for online shopping

d. What do people consider while buying clothes online?

Design and product quality os considered by 38% of the shoppers. Brand value is chosen by 21% and price and discount is the reason that 41% people prefer online over offline shopping. This can be seen in figure 4.5.

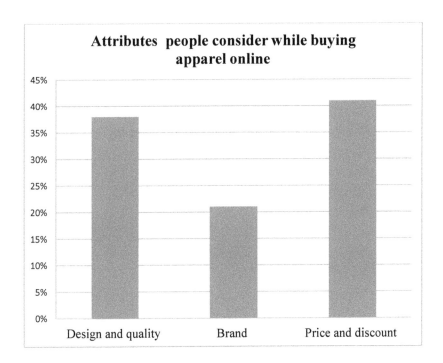

Figure 4.5 Attributes people consider while buying apparel online

e. **Have you ever returned any garment bought online? If yes, what were the reasons?**

The main reasons of return were as follows:

a. Size and fit problem being 42%.

b. Product being defective attributing to 21%.

c. Fabric quality accounting to 19%.

d. Product delivered not being the same as shown contributing to 10%.

e. Colour difference issues being 8%.

The analysis is shown in figure 4.6.

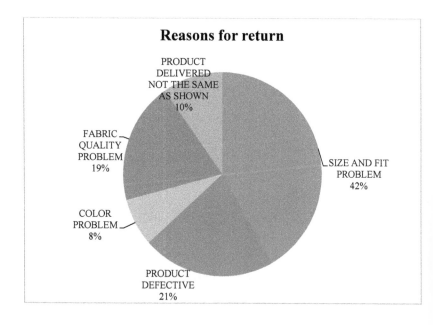

Figure 4.6 Reasons for return

f. What all attributes can be included to make online shopping experience better?

39% of the customers suggested that a video explaining the unique selling point of the garment or designer's point of view would help in a better understanding the garment well. 30% also chose that a three dimensional view or 360 degree view would also contribute. 31% felt the need for a virtual fitting solution that would also assist in finding the right fit for the garment. The analysis is shown in figure 4.7.

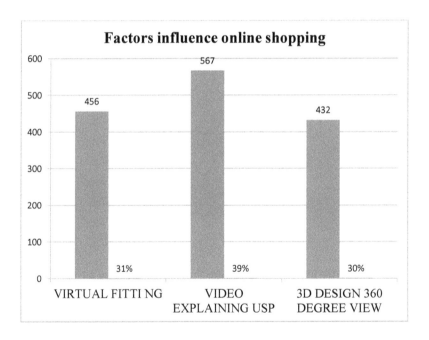

Figure 4.7 Factors influence online shopping

g. What all attributes can make online shopping better and improved?

The analysis suggests that 33% of the customers selected 3D design/360 degree view. Try and buy option is preferred by 30%, customization of size by 19% and the availability of colour swatch at the time of ordering is favoured by 18%. The analysis is shown in figure 4.8.

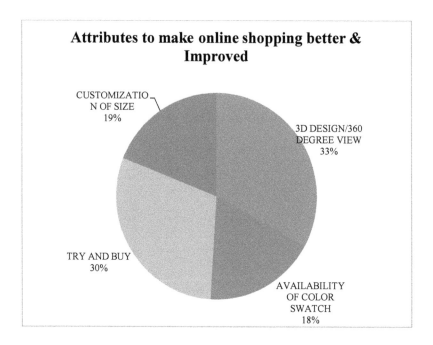

Figure 4.8 Attributes to make online shopping better and improved

h. Do customers think that if a video describing the creation and the unique selling points of the garment, that explains designer's point of view will help in better understanding of the garment?

83% of the customers agreed that video describing unique selling point of the garment will really help in understanding the garment better. The results are shown in figure 4.9.

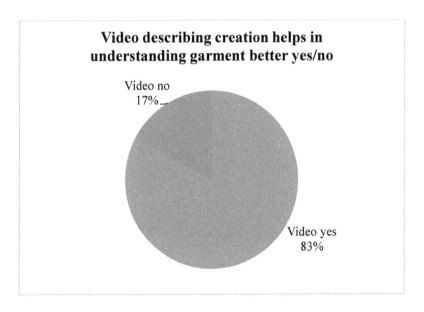

Figure 4.9 Video describing the garment creation helps in understanding garment better

i. **Having understood the virtual fitting solution, what would the customer prefer?**

65% of customers agreed that a virtual fitting solution can really help in understanding the fit of the garment as shown in figure 4.10.

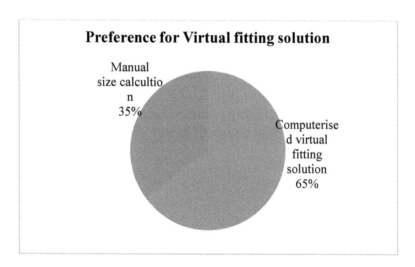

Figure 4.10 Preference for virtual fitting solution

4.2.1 Correlation between various attributes

The correlation between various attributes was done using "R" software. The results are as follows:

4.2.1.1 The correlation between the attributes and their impact where people shifted from online buying to offline buying in the last six months.

The results helped analyse the reasons for the radical shift from online to offline shopping in the last six months. The ability to check the correct size and fit from an offline store was the most significant factor. The same people required to feel the fabric and also wanted the apparel to be available to them at the time of purchase.

The concordance was 61%.

There is a very strong and intuitive story that gets unraveled here. Looking at the odds ratio to compare the impact of each variable, the chances that number of shoppers will switch from online to offline increased because of the following reasons:

Color problem experienced: log (2.12)

Product not the same as shown: log (1.8)

Fabric quality: log (1.7)

Similarly, comfort of getting the delivery of the product at the point of purchase increases the chances of them shifting from online to offline by log(1.37), followed by ability to check the apparel for size and fit by log (1.33) and getting touch and feel of the fabric by log (1.22).The detailed workings of these results are shown in Annexure-I.

4.2.1.2 The correlation between the attributes and their impact where people shifted from offline to online shopping of apparel.

Discounts and home delivery were clearly the two significant factors. The same people seemed to find size charts reliable. However they thought, that a video describing the creation and the unique selling point of the garment, that explains designers point of view will help in better understanding of the garment.

The concordance is 66%.

A video describing the creation and the unique selling points of the garment, that explains designer's point of view will help in better understanding of the apparel will also increase the chances of shifting from offline to online by log (1.9).

Size chart reliability increases their chances of shifting from offline to online by log (1.7).

Discounted/lower prices available on online will increase their chances of shifting to online by log (1.4).

Further home delivery also increases their chances of shifting from offline to online by log (1.2). The detailed workings of these results are shown in Annexure-II.

4.2.1.3 The correlation between the attributes and their impact on people, who shop online.

People adopt online shopping for the reason that the product is delivered at their door step. It is also picked for the reliability of its size chart.

They feel that a video describing the creation, and the unique selling points of the garment, that explains designer's point of view will help in better understanding of the garment. They prefer virtual fitting solution for the size and fit.

The concordance is 63%.

Now when we look at the odds ratio to compare the impact of each variable.

People who shop online for apparel:

Size chart reliability has made people shop online by log (1.63).

A video describing the creation, the unique selling points of the garment, and the designer's point of view will help in better understanding of the garment and also help people shop online by log (1.63).

The provision of virtual fitting over manual size calculation can also impact people to shop online by log (1.47).

Home delivery has also impacted people to shop online by log (1.21). The detailed workings of these results are shown in Annexure-III.

4.2.1.4 Summary

The key reasons why customers shopped from a physical store were the ability to check the garment for size and fit, experience the feel of the fabric followed by gratification of immediacy which is to get the product at the same instance. Other reasons rated lower down the order were the attractiveness of display and visual merchandising and ability to speak with the store manager in the stores. However, those who prefer to buy online, the primary driver being discount/lower price (64%) followed by unavailability of the product in physical store (15%) and the rest for gifting and sending outstation.

For those who bought online, the key considerations while making a purchase decision were price & discount (41%), design & quality (38%) followed by Brand name (21%).

Further, shoppers who shop online primarily for price & discount, a whopping 74% were of the view that to make their experience better 3-D design/360 degree view and computerized virtual fitting solution can play an important role. A possible video describing the creation and the unique selling points of the garment that explains designer's point of view will help in better understanding of the garment said 83% of the respondents.

42% of these shoppers had actually returned the garment because of size and fit problem.

Those shopping online felt that following features will improve the online shopping experience:

a. 3D design/360 view: 33%

b. Computerized virtual fitting solution: 65%

c. Video describing the creation and the unique selling points of the garment that explains designer's point of view will help in better understanding of the garment: 83%.

d. They prefer to search for their apparel by typing the category : 57% followed by clicking on the picture : 43%

4.3 ANALYSIS OF OFFLINE STUDY DONE AT VARIOUS BRICK AND MORTAR STORES

4.3.1 Identification of attributes to the problem of size and fit

A study was also conducted at various offline stores in Bangalore for identification of attributes related to the problem of size and fit of the garments. The study was conducted by observation and through conduction of personal interviews with 100 customers. The result for problems faced in women's top-wear category and Indian ethnic-wear (Kurta) are shown in figure 4.11 and figure 4.12 respectively.

It has been observed that if a female customer is of size 'S', she would want to try the garment in case of any exceptions before making a purchase.

in an offline scenario she would carry sizes "S", "XS" and "M" to the trial room due to lack of surety in the believed size of the specific brand. In India, there is no standard size chart and each brand has its own. The customers try the apparel and show the fit to their accompanying friends, mothers or spouses. If a customer chooses a bigger size, the fit changes in all the other areas. With some designs where the chest and the waist were loose, it has been observed that the customers were satisfied with the fit and those designs were preferred the most.

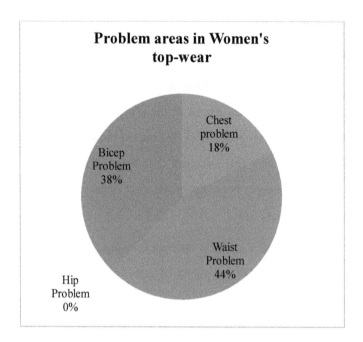

Figure 4.11 Problem areas in women's top-wear in a physical store

Problem areas in women's wear top-wear analyzed are shown in table 4.2.

Table 4.2 Problem areas in Women's top-wear

Fit problem around chest	18%
Problem with Bicep area	38%
Problem in the waist area	44%

The analysis for women's wear Kurta are shown in figure 4.12.

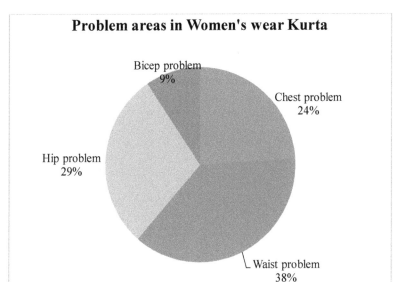

Figure 4.12 Problem areas women's wear straight kurta in a physical store

The problems identified in the study for ethnic wear kurta are shown in table 4.3.

Table 4.3 Problem areas in women's wear Kurta category

Fit problem around chest	24%
Problem with Bicep area	9%
Problem in the waist area	38%
Problem around hip area	29%

4.3.2 Summary

It can be concluded that the problem areas in women's wear were mainly Chest, Waist, Hip and Biceps. The study focuses the attention on how these elements can be taken care of and how the fit can be made flexible.

4.4 ANALYSIS OF THE STUDY DONE AT FLIPKART

The data collected from Flipkart for three months from Dec 2014 to Feb 2015 was analyzed. The results are shown in table 4.4.

Table 4.4 Major Reasons for Return

S.NO.	REASON	DEC RETURNS	JAN RETURNS	FEB RETURNS	Total	%
1	FABRIC QUALITY	10468	12862	17299	40629	24.79%
2	SIZE_NOT_AS_EXPECTED	11854	13473	13792	39119	23.86%
3	FIT_NOT_AS_EXPECTED	8951	10065	10889	29905	18.24%
4	COLOR_DO_NOT_LIKE_NOT_AS_EXPECTED	7138	8193	10165	25496	15.55%
5	DAMAGED_PRODUCT_RECEIVED	2848	2960	3727	9535	5.82%
6	ORDERED_A_RECEIVED_B	2129	2396	3054	7579	4.62%
7	STITCH	914	1147	1387	3448	2.10%
8	MISSING_PRODUCT	749	694	652	2095	1.28%
9	SPECIFICATION_ERROR	507	557	973	2037	1.24%
10	CUSTOMER_DOES_NOT_WANT	557	507	557	1621	0.99%
11	MISSING_ACCESSORY	195	218	323	736	0.45%
12	AFTER_WASH	168	212	260	640	0.39%
13	HANDLE_STRAP_ISSUES	57	108	103	268	0.16%
14	ZIP_ISSUE	66	75	76	217	0.13%
15	WRONG_PRODUCT_ORDERED	44	44	55	143	0.09%
16	BELT_BUCKLE_ISSUES	43	43	42	128	0.08%
17	DAMAGED_OUTER_PACKAGE_RECEIVED	39	39	44	122	0.07%
18	MISSING_FREEBIE	24	37	51	112	0.07%
19	TAMPERED_SEAL	20	38	34	92	0.06%
	Total	46771	53668	63483	163922	100.00%

The four major problematic areas found in the analysis are shown in figure 4.13.

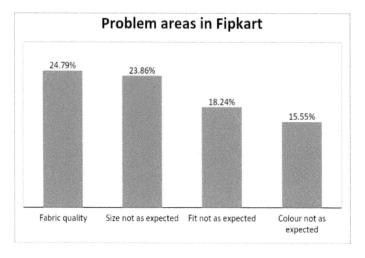

Figure 4.13 Major problem areas in Flipkart

The problem areas analysed are as follows:

- Fabric quality 24.79%
- Size not as expected 23.86%
- Fit not as expected 18.24%
- Colour not as expected 15.55%

4.5 ANALYSIS OF STUDY DONE WITH VARIOUS ECOMMERCE COMPANIES

4.5.1 Study at Snapdeal

The data analysis of study done at Snapdeal is shown in figure 4.14.

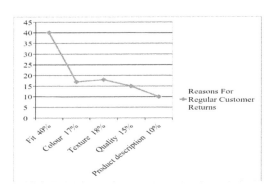

Figure 4.14 Reasons for return in Snapdeal

- According to study, 40 % of garments were returned because of fit problems.
- 17% of the customers had issues with the colour.
- 10% of the garments were returned because of product description was not adequate.
- 18% were returned as they failed to meet the quality standards of the garment.

4.5.2 Study at Fashionara

The analysis of the study is shown in figure 4.14.

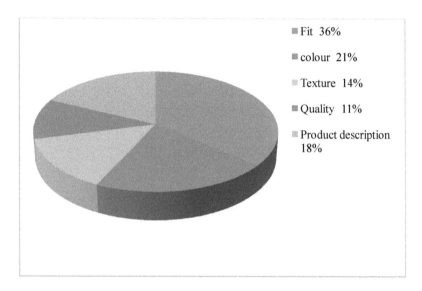

Figure 4.15 Reasons for return in Fashionara

4.5.3. Study at 100bestbuy

The reasons for return are shown in table 4.5.

Table 4.5 Reasons for return at 100bestbuy

Size problem	10.71%
Fit problem	14.30%
Colour problem	7.14%
Wrong Product	25%
Quality issues	25%
Display problem	7.14%
Product delivered not the same	10.71%

4.5.4 Study at Myntra

Reasons for return are as follows:

- 10-12 % of the rejections average of internal and external brands.
- 50-60 % of returns are because of sizing issues (Nike follows US size chart, Puma follows UK size chart).
- 5-10 % of returns are because the fabric quality failed to meet the customer's expectation.
- Washes is a new problem that comes across to customers as a defect in the garment.
- 10% of returns were due to disparity in colour seen and colour received.(colour not as seen on the web page).

4.6 SUMMARY OF THE STUDY

The analysis has been summarized in the table 4.6.

Table 4.6 Summary of the study

Attributes	Survey	Flipkart	Snap deal	Fashionara	100best buy	Myntra	Avg %
Fabric quality	19%	24.79	18%	14%	-	10%	17%
Size not as Expected	21%	23.86%	-	-	10.71%	12%	17%
Fit not as expected	21%	18.24%	40%	36%	14.3%	-	26%
Colour not as expected	8%	15.55%	17%	21%	7.14%	10%	13%
Product Description	-	1.24%	10%	18%	-	-	10%
Quality	21%	5.82%	15%	11%	25%		16%

From the analysis, it can be concluded that the questionable areas in apparel are size:17% and fit: 26%. The colour problem comprise 13% and product description forms 10% of all the areas identified. The fabric quality constitutes 17% and product quality amounts to 16%. The researcher has to work in these areas of concern. The next chapter elaborates the recommendations to the above mentioned problems.

CHAPTER 5

RECOMMENDATIONS

The previous chapters identified the main challenges faced by the customers. Through the course of this chapter new solutions have been recommended in each of the three problem areas. These solutions aim to improve consumer experience and strengthen the perspective of shopping online.

5.1 SIZE AND FIT

The problem of size and fit can be solved by making a small change in the existing online size chart. If the sizing table elaborating the body type can be slightly modified by adding ease amounts to the bust and hips, it will impact the garment returns rates to quite an extent.

5.1.1 New size chart

A new scientific size chart is recommended. Size chart would constitute all the elements and attributes required to understand the chosen garment well. It would also include sizes of UK / USA / Europe for easy comparison and explicit understanding. The size chart would clearly remark whether it references the measurements of the actual garment or the of the human body. This lack of clarity in existing size charts have created a paradox and trust deficits between the buyer and the seller. The proposed size chart is shown in table 5.1.

Table 5.1 Size chart for women's wear top

Size	XS	S	M	L
Euro Size	34	36	38	41
Bust/Chest	32-33.4	33.5-35.4	35.5-37.4	37.5-41
Waist	27.5-30.5	30.6-32.5	32.6-34.5	34.6-36.5
Shoulder	14	14.5	15	15.5
Sleeves length	22	20.5	21	21.5
Length	25	26	26	26.5

Note: Size chart as per body measurements.

The size chart should be such that it should distinctly define that the size 34 covers body measurements till 33.4 inches and any measurement bigger than that would pertain to the next size. This should also include whether the measurements given are the body measurements or the actual measurements of the garment. The attributes which are important for understanding the garment such as various measurements like chest, waist, shoulder, hip, sleeves length and length of the garment should be clearly defined to understand the size better are shown in table 5.2.

Table 5.2 Size chart with all the important attributes

Sizes	XS	S	M	L	XL	XXL
U.K.	6	8	10	12	14	16
U.S.A.	2	4	6	8	10	12
Euro	34	36	38	40	42	44
Bust	34"	36"	39"	42"	45"	47"
Waist	33"	35"	38"	41"	44"	46"
Shoulder	14"	14.5"	15"	15.5"	16"	16.5"
Hip	37"	38"	39"	40"	41"	42"
3/4th Sleeves	17"	17.5"	17.5"	18"	18"	18.5"
Full Sleeves	20"	20.5"	21"	21.5"	22"	22.5"

Note: Size chart as per the garment measurements.

5.1.2 Design thinking

The garment that can be sold online on long term basis sustainably needs to be designed uniquely and constructed as compared to what sells offline as its design needs to offset qualities of touch, feel and ornateness.

Garments designed to be sold online need to be thought differently. It should be designed in such a way that it offsets problems of size and fit. The garments hence designed need to keep in mind the key areas of fit such as chest, waist and bicep to cater to those who buy online as they would not get an opportunity to try it out unlike in an offline store to identify the issue of fit.

To address the problems mentioned above, the next step was to construct ideas that were meaningful yet functional for online business.

5.1.2.1 Creative Ideas

To solve the problem of size and fit, the following design ideas are recommended:

- **The sleeve-bodice combinations design**

    The sleeve and top of any garment (blouse, dress, jacket, or coat) can be combined in a variety of ways categorized as follows:

    a. Kimono designs.
    b. Kaftan designs.
    c. Raglan designs.
    d. Drop shoulder designs or deep-cut armhole designs.

a. **Kimono designs:** The total sleeve combines or is all-in-one with the top garment as shown in figure 5.1.

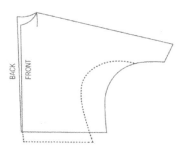

Figure 5.1 Kimono sleeves

b. **Kaftan designs:** The design is loose garment with long wide sleeves as shown in figure 5.2.

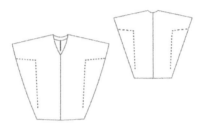

Figure 5.2 Kaftan Sleeve

c. **Raglan designs:** The raglan sleeve pattern is developed by including part of the neckline and armhole to complete the sleeve draft (Joseph-Armstrong, Helen., 2007). The raglan can be designed for bodice, dress, blouse, jackets, coats and other garments. The sleeve combines with part of an armhole and shoulder area of the apparel as shown in figure 5.3.

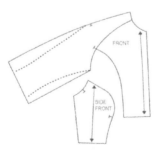

Figure 5.3 Raglan sleeves

d.   Drop-shoulder designs: The drop shoulder pattern is developed by attaching a portion of the upper sleeve cap to the bodice. The dropped shoulder extends beyond the shoulder tip and covers part of the upper arm at varying lengths as shown in figure 5.4. The garment can be developed with or without the lower sleeve, or the lower sleeve can be attached to the garment. The design can be applied to dresses, blouses, jackets, coats, active wear, evening dresses and so on (Joseph-Armstrong, Helen., 2007).

Figure 5.4 Drop Shoulder short sleeves

- **Other choices can be as follows:**

    ● **Deep-cut armhole designs:** The armhole section of a bodice combines with sleeves (Joseph-Armstrong, Helen., 2007).

    Each of the combination patterns can be used to develop innovative design variations where there can be a lot of scope for fitting the same garment to various body types.

- **Combining knitted fabric with the woven fabric to give fit flexibility**

    Fit flexibility can be provided by using a combination of fabrics which have certain amount of stretch or elasticity. A few inch variations in size at chest and sleeve area can also be taken care by combining knitted fabrics.

5.1.2.2 A garment is designed and fully constructed as part of this research

The garment is created using Kaftan sleeves which allows scope for variations in chest measurements and the waist is made flexible which can be adjusted by the buyer themself according to their choice of fit. The specifications of the garment are shown in figure 5.5.

There are three fitting choices given around the waist by providing an adjustable button at the back that can be adjusted with respect to the type of fit a customer demands. The choice could be loose or tight and also the button can be left open if the choice is really loose or casual fit is demanded around the waist.

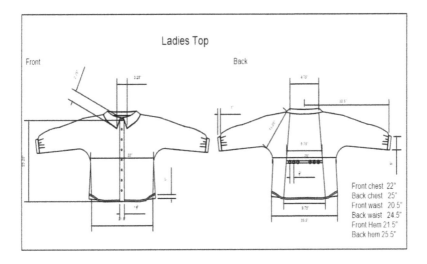

Figure 5.5 Specifications of the front and back of the garment created

The front and back side of the actual garment is shown in figure 5.6. The adjustable buttons at the back side are shown in figure 5.7. How the actual garment will look with and without closing the adjustable buttons is shown in figure 5.8.

Figure 5.6 Front and back side of the top with adjustable button

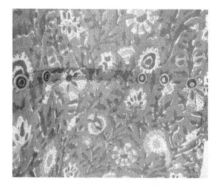

Figure 5.7 Adjustable buttons at the back side of the top provided with 3 options to adjust the fit

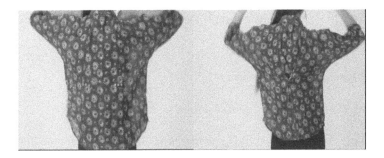

Figure 5.8 Actual garment without closing the adjustable buttons and with closed buttons

5.1.2.3 Testing of the garment created

A combination of subjective fit trials and objective fit trials were used to test the garments. In subjective fit trials, the subjects from the target population were asked to try on the test garments. The innovative garments created were tested on 100 people in Bangalore where the customers were the same size but with different body shapes. The feedback was collected and analyzed. The garments created could fit 90% of the population of the same size for different body shapes.

It can be concluded from the results that if garments can be created in such a way that it could fit many people of the same size with different body shapes, then the problem of fit and size can be resolved.

5.1.3 Online trial room

A comprehensive online trial room solution on the website would allow customers to support their buying decision in a very effective way. By providing the customers with an actual way of visualizing the fit of the garment would enhance the buying process significantly. They will be able to ask for their friend's opinion to help them with their decisions by a simple click of a button on social-media.

5.1.3.1 Recommended software

Making of a virtual fitting room solution

The objective of the virtual fitting room is to let the customers see the fit of the garment.

- A table is made with all possible combinations of sizes of a human body
- An e-mannequin, is constructed where its chest, waist and neck could be adjusted to various possible size combinations electronically via a computer.
- The e-mannequin was adjusted to each possible combination of the table and a photograph was taken with the garment fitted on e-mannequin covering all the angles.
- When the buyer enters their own measurements in the Interactive trial room, they will see an image showing the fit of the garment they have selected for the size measurement they have entered along with the fit advice. The advice will show how the chest fits or the waist will fit. Example: Recommended size M ,waist is comfort fit, chest is loose by 2 inches and so on.

Further, an algorithm for an online trial room is presented. The right fit is not as simple as description, or set of numbers, or sizing; it is an emotional decision that someone perceives as 'looking good' on them. Some people want to wear a particular shirt fitted closely, while another person may want to wear the same shirt but fitted loosely.

A visual demonstration of fit, an exclusive way to show how a certain size will look on their body type is the only way to give shoppers the confidence they need to purchase, secure in the knowledge they are unlikely to need to return the garment for reasons of fit. The goal is to enable everyone to see how clothes will fit them.

- A size chart is created (it contains a list of all the combination of different body parameters for which photos have to be taken for a particular garment of a particular style and size).
- A mannequin, that contorts to different body shapes, is introduced, on which garments are worn according to the size chart created.
- A considerable number of photos, covering all the angles, are taken for each garment and size, so that when customers input their measurements in the online trial room software running on the website, they'll see a photo of the mannequin with their measurements, wearing the garment they've chosen, in the size and style that they've chosen.
- The customer would be able to see the fit by looking at the pictures of the front and back side of the garment. The fit advice will also be provided which will be given by showing by how much inches the waist will be tight or loose or by how much inches chest will be tight or loose. Whether the garment is a comfort fit, loose fit or tight fit will also be mentioned. The customer will also be able to edit the body measurements. The customer would also be able to try various sizes for the body measurements given at one time only.

Recommended virtual fitting Algorithm is shown in figure 5.9.

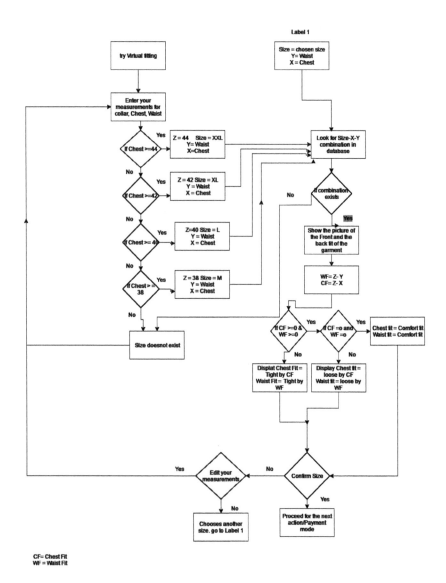

Figure 5.9 Recommended virtual fitting Algorithm

5.1.3.2 Application Development

- The Interactive trial room application can be hosted online using Apache Server version 8.14
- The software is made using PHP and JavaScript.
- The backend consists of MySQL database which contains the required attributes along with all the clicked pictures of garment worn on the e-mannequin.

STEP 1:

Make a table consisting of size chart with all the possible size variations as shown in Table 5.3. The various waist combinations for a particular chest size "M" has been created as follows:

Table 5.3 Size chart for size Medium with chest 40 inches and all waist combinations from 35 inches to 43 inches

Size	Chest in inches	Waist in inches
M	40	35
M	40	36
M	40	37
M	40	38
M	40	39
M	40	40
M	40	41
M	40	42
M	40	43

STEP 2:

- The next step is to permute the e-mannequin to the various size combinations as per table 5.3 via a computer. The e-mannequin is set for size 'M' with chest size at 40 inches and waist at 35 inches .The garment with size 40 is portrayed on the e-mannequin and pictures are clicked for the front as well as the back roundabout of the garment as draped on e-mannequin. This will help consumer aniticipate the fit of the garment and also to comprehend how the garment drapes. The above activity is repeated this time for chest constant at 40 and the waist adjusted from 36 inches to 43 inches. The same process is done for all the other sizes like L(large) and the e-mannequin set for chest size at 42 inches and all the waist combinations from 35 inches to 43 inches. The process is repeated for XL(Extra Large) size with chest fixed at 44 and waist adjusted from 35 inches to 43 inches and 2XL(2 Extra Large) with chest at 46 and waist adjusted from 35 inches to 43 inches. The pictures are clicked for the front side as well as the rear side of garment draped on the e-mannequin.

STEP 3:

- The backend database will be created using MySQL which will contain data with main attributes like size-chest-waist combinations along with the images clicked for that particular size for the front and the back as shown in Table 5.4.

Table 5.4 Database for size Medium with chest 40 and all the combinations for the waist from 30 inches to 40 inches along with the images clicked for the front and the back side of the garment

Size	Chest in inches	Waist in inches	Picture-number for the Front and Back side of the garment
M	40	30	M-40-30-front
			M-40-30-back
M	40	31	M-40-31-front
			M-40-31-back
M	40	32	M-40-32-front
			M-40-32-back
M	40	33	M-40-33-front
			M-40-33-back
M	40	34	M-40-34-front
			M-40-34-back
M	40	35	M-40-35-front
			M-40-35-back
M	40	36	M-40-36-front
			M-40-36-back
M	40	37	M-40-37-front
			M-40-37-back
M	40	38	M-40-38-front
			M-40-38-back
M	40	39	M-40-39-front
			M-40-39-back
M	40	40	M-40-40-front
			M-40-40-back

Table 5.5 Database for size Medium with chest 39 and all the combinations for the waist from 28 inches to 40 inches along with the images clicked for the front and the back side of the garment

Size	Chest in inches	Waist in inches	Picture-number for the Front and Back side of the garment
M	39	40	M-39-40-front
			M-39-40-back
M	39	39	M-39-39-front
			M-39-39-back
M	39	38	M-39-38-front
			M-39-38-back
M	39	37	M-39-37-front
			M-39-37-back
M	39	36	M-39-36-front
			M-39-36-back
M	39	35	M-39-35-front
			M-39-35-back
M	39	34	M-39-34-front
			M-39-34-back
M	39	33	M-39-33-front
			M-39-33-back
M	39	32	M-39-32-front
			M-39-32-back
M	39	31	M-39-31-front
			M-39-31-back
M	39	30	M-39-30-front
			M-39-30-back
M	39	29	M-39-29-front
			M-39-29-back
M	39	28	M-39-28-front
			M-39-28-back

Table 5.6 Database for size Medium with chest 38 and all the combinations for the waist from 28 inches to 39 inches along with the images clicked for the front and the back side of the garment

Size	Chest in inches	Waist in inches	Picture-number for the Front and Back side of the garment
M	38	39	M-38-39-front
			M-38-39-back
M	38	38	M-38-38-front
			M-38-38-back
M	38	37	M-38-37-front
			M-38-37-back
M	38	36	M-38-36-front
			M-38-36-back
M	38	35	M-38-35-front
			M-38-35-back
M	38	34	M-38-34-front
			M-38-34-back
M	38	33	M-38-33-front
			M-38-33-back
M	38	32	M-38-32-front
			M-38-32-back
M	38	31	M-38-31-front
			M-38-31-back
M	38	30	M-38-30-front
			M-38-30-back
M	38	29	M-38-29-front
			M-38-29-back
M	38	28	M-38-28-front
			M-38-28-back

Table 5.7 Database for size Medium with chest 37 and all the combinations for the waist from 28 inches to 36 inches along with the images clicked for the front and the back side of the garment

Size	Chest in inches	Waist in inches	Picture-number for the Front and Back side of the garment
M	37	36	M-37-36-front
			M-37-36-back
M	37	35	M-37-35-front
			M-37-35-back
M	37	34	M-37-34-front
			M-37-34-back
M	37	33	M-37-33-front
			M-37-33-back
M	37	32	M-37-32-front
			M-37-32-back
M	37	31	M-37-31-front
			M-37-31-back
M	37	30	M-37-30-front
			M-37-30-back
M	37	29	M-37-29-front
			M-37-29-back
M	37	28	M-37-28-front
			M-37-28-back

Table 5.8 Database for size Medium with chest 36 and all the combinations for the waist from 28 inches to 36 inches along with the images clicked for the front and the back side of the garment

Size	Chest in inches	Waist in inches	Picture-number for the Front and Back side of the garment
M	36	36	M-36-36-front
			M-36-36-back
M	36	35	M-36-35-front
			M-36-35-back
M	36	34	M-36-34-front
			M-36-34-back
M	36	33	M-36-33-front
			M-36-33-back
M	36	32	M-36-32-front
			M-36-32-back
M	36	31	M-36-31-front
			M-36-31-back
M	36	30	M-36-30-front
			M-36-30-back
M	36	29	M-36-29-front
			M-36-29-back
M	36	28	M-36-28-front
			M-36-28-back

Table 5.9 Database for size Medium with chest 35 and all the combinations for the waist from 28 inches to 34 inches along with the images clicked for the front and back side of the garment

Size	Chest in inches	Waist in inches	Picture-number for the Front and Back side of the garment
M	35	34	M-35-34-front
			M-35-34-back
M	35	33	M-35-33-front
			M-35-33-back
M	35	32	M-35-32-front
			M-35-32-back
M	35	31	M-35-31-front
			M-35-31-back
M	35	30	M-35-30-front
			M-35-30-back
M	35	29	M-35-29-front
			M-35-29-back
M	35	28	M-35-28-front
			M-35-28-back

Table 5.10 Database for size Medium with chest 34 and all the combinations for the waist from 28 inches to 33 inches along with the images clicked for the front and the back side of the garment

Size	Chest in inches	Waist in inches	Picture-number for the Front and Back side of the garment
M	34	33	M-34-33-front
			M-34-33-back
M	34	32	M-34-32-front
			M-34-32-back
M	34	31	M-34-31-front
			M-34-31-back
M	34	30	M-34-30-front
			M-34-30-back
M	34	29	M-34-29-front
			M-34-29-back
M	34	28	M-34-28-front
			M-34-28-back

- The same process is done for the other sizes like Large, Extra Large and Double extra large .The data is collected and pictures are clicked for various permutations of the front and the back for similar chest and waist combinations.
- **The source code for the product is available in Annexure 4.**

5.1.3.3 Working of Virtual fitting room

The front page of the actual application is shown in figure 5.11.

Figure 5.11 Front page of actual application

- The customer enters the application by clicking on "Virtual fitting room" button
- The customer will be asked to enter a few body measurements:

Enter the body measurements in inches.

- Collar:
- Chest:
- Waist:
- Customer clicks on the proceed button to start the application

  The actual application page which will open and ask for the body measurements is shown in figure 5.12

Figure 5.12 Measurement page of the actual application

The buyer will give the body measurements as shown in figure 5.13 and then can press the proceed button to check the virtual fit of the garment selected.

Figure 5.13 Measurement page with proceed button

- The application looks for the best combination with respect to the entered measurements from the database. If the combination is available then the image of that garment is shown for the front and the back view along with the appropriate fit advice. For instance, the recommended size is 38 for the body measurements entered. The recommended size and the fit advice would be shown as shown in figure 5.14.

Figure 5.14 Fit advice as per the body measurements given

If the buyer likes the fit, they can confirm size else they can continue to try the next set of sizes based on their conjecture. If the buyer chooses size 40, then the fit for the selected size will be shown as shown in figure 5.15.

Figure 5.15 Fit advice if chosen size is 40.

If customer chooses the next size to try say, size 42 then the fit advice will be given accordingly as shown in figure 5.16. The customer can see how various sizes will fit on him and the advice respectively.

Figure 5.16 Fit advice if chosen size is 42

Figure 5.17 Fit advice if chosen size is 44

The process continues till the time the customer would like to try different sizes and is also satisfied with the fit. If the customer wants, there is an option to edit body measurements and go through the "Virtual fitting solution" again.

The Interactive trial room mechanism will help the customer to understand the fit of the garment along with the drape of the garment on the individual's body. The customers can try all possible sizes for the fit to reassure themselves the suitable fit before completing the purchase. This will help the customer take the accurate decision before selecting the ordered size and provide them with better understanding of the fit of the chosen garment.

- **The source code for the fit advice is shown in Annexure 5.**
- **The source code for How to get measurements from the customer is shown in Annexure 5.**

5.1.3.4 Summary

The Interactive trial room solution can help customers to virtually try the garment and assure themselves of the fit and has the potential to reduce returns.

This will improve customer satisfaction and over a period of time reduce the problem of merchandise returns that has been plaguing fashion apparel ecommerce business.

5.2 COLOUR SOLUTION

5.2.1 Understanding the importance of colour

Colour is defined as the property controlled by a protest of delivering diverse sensations on the eye subsequently of the way it reflects or discharges light. it is likewise the most chameleon-like. It is very baffling to find a mismatch between what you order and what you get, no matter where it may be. When a corporate logo turns out green instead of teal, when a t-shirt is returned because it's not tomato red, the attitude is quite different.

With the large number of e-commerce transactions that involve fashion and apparel, a comprehensive set of information needs to be mentioned and elaborated on the website for the consumers to note. Colour represents one of them. Colour information can consist of both verbal information (e.g. a description of a product as being royal blue) and the Pantone number.

5.2.3 Solutions to Colour complications

To overcome the problem of colour few suggestions have been made:

5.2.3.1 Pantone colour matching system

The Pantone Colour Matching System is largely a standardized colour reproduction system. By standardizing the colours, different manufacturers in different locations can all refer to the Pantone system to make sure colours match without direct contact with one another.

One such use is standardizing colours in the CMYK process. The CMYK process is a method of printing colour by using four inks—cyan, magenta, yellow, and black. A majority of the world's printed material is produced using the CMYK process, and there is a special subset of Pantone colours that can be reproduced using CMYK. One such use is standardizing colours in the CMYK process. The CMYK process is a method of printing colour by using four inks—cyan, magenta, yellow, and black. A majority of the world's printed material is produced using the CMYK process, and there is a special subset of Pantone colours that can be reproduced using CMYK.

5.2.3.2 Implementation of Pantone code

The mismatch of colours between screen and actual garment can be resolved by making an innovative use of Pantone code for every colour. The seller will provide the colour description as well as the Pantone reference code for every apparel to give a better understanding about the colour. This description will be present along with the garment that the customer is looking to buy.

Pantone process colour numbers start with the letter p followed by a one- to three-digit number, a dash, and a one- to two-digit number. The "c" suffix indicates coated stock and the "u" uncoated. There exist paper, cotton, and nylon guides and standard colour reference numbers in this system contain two digits followed by a dash and four digits with either a tpx or tcx suffix. tpx indicates that that the reference was produced on paper, the tcx indicates that it's a dyed cotton reference. Each colour also has a descriptive name reference as a secondary identifier.

The Pantone colour details will be provided to the customer with the packaging of the first garment delivered. The product description page on the website will explicitly mention the Pantone colour code of the garment under consideration. Using the Pantone code, the customer can reassure the colour by matching the code with the exact colour on the previously delivered packaging material. This will remove any discordance between the selected colour versus the colour delivered.

A Pantone colour swatch will be provided to the customer as shown in figure 5.18.

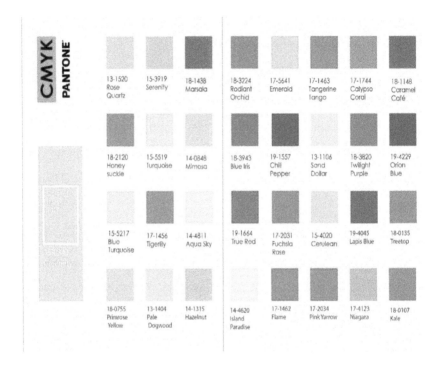

Figure 5.18 Pantone code colour swatch

Following the posting of the swatches. The customer will have full realisation of how the colour in future purchased garments will be.

The colour of the garment will also be shown along with the Pantone code in the website as shown below in figure 5.19.

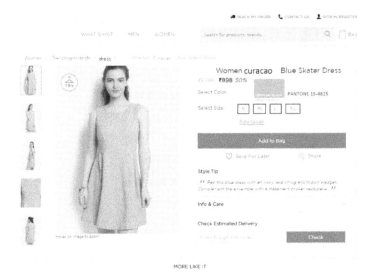

Figure 5.19 Recommended Solution with implemented pantone code

This will be implemented across the various e-commerce websites to provide the customers the real satisfaction and to avoid any future return efforts.

The other colours that the garment is made in will follow the same pantone policy.

Hence, various colour options for the same garment should be included in the same web page along with the Pantone code as shown below in figure 5.6

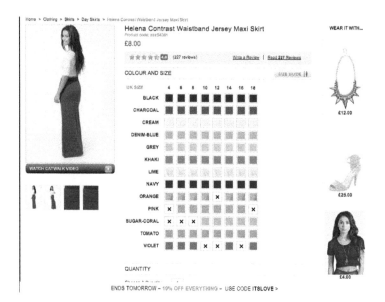

Figure 5.20 Garments with all the available colours can be shown on the same page

This is one of the ways which would lead to supreme customer contentment and would contribute a lot towards realizing the true spirit of e-commerce in its very native form.

5.3 PRODUCT DESCRIPTION

5.3.1 Introduction

The important attributes of a garment description should be defined clearly. It should be mentioned whether the garment is semi stitched or unstitched should be clearly mentioned.

A comprehensive set of detailed product attributes are recommended, which if included will offer a supreme experience to customers while buying online.

5.3.2 The important attributes to describe a garment are mentioned below:

- Material
- Length of the garment
- Wash care
- Touch and feel
- Colour, size chart
- Return policy, delivery time and any value added.

5.3.2.1 Material

The description of the material such as fabric details play an important role in making a good selection of the garment. The material description should cover the following:

The composition of the fabric as well as the thread count of the fabric. Some of the examples are as follows:

- Material: 100 % Cotton, Thread Count: 220
- Material: 80% cotton & 20% Polyester.
- Material : georgette, weight: 80grams.
- Material Rayon
- Transparency of the fabric : not transparent
- lining material : none
- print & pattern : stripes or print
- work : lace or embroidery

These attributes can help the customer to understand the apparel better.

An example is shown in figure 5.21 below.

Figure 5.21 An example of description

5.3.2.1.1. Recommendation for indication of fabric thickness

The thickness of the fabric is not known to the customer till they receive the garment/s. Hence the chances of returning it are more due to the fabric being inclined towards a sheer side being different from their expectation.

To solve this issue, the grams per square meter of the garment, the metric measurement of the weight of a fabric (GSM) for every fabric can be collected and can be added to the garment's respective description.

This can be used as a parameter to establish a clear relationship between GSM and thickness which can be given to the customer in the form of a thickened meter or indicator which suggests the fabric. The GSM of the fabric will be read from the description, The GSM will be compared with the database stored for each GSM and the transparency level. The thickness guide meter will be shown accordingly, which can help customers to understand the thickness or the quality of the fabric and also guide whether an inner layer is need or not. The recommendation is shown in figure 5.22.

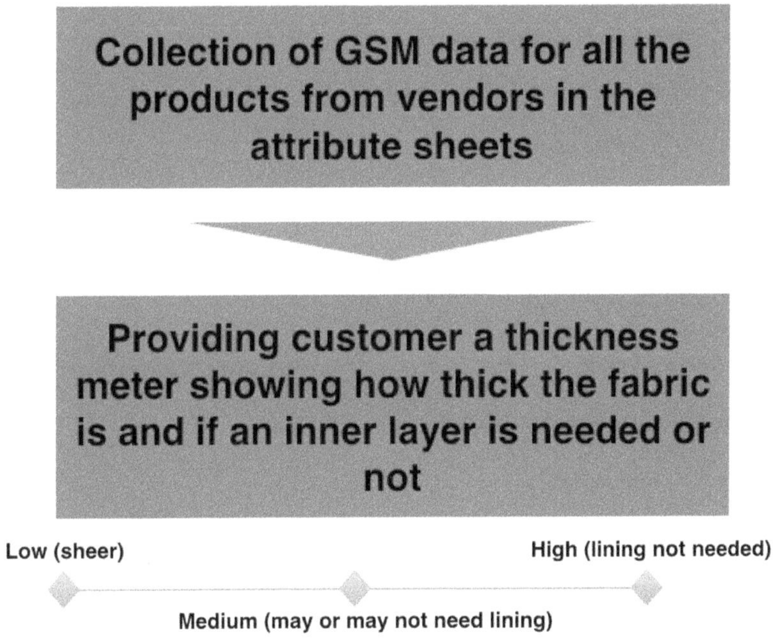

Collection of GSM data for all the products from vendors in the attribute sheets

⬇

Providing customer a thickness meter showing how thick the fabric is and if an inner layer is needed or not

Low (sheer)   High (lining not needed)

Medium (may or may not need lining)

Figure 5.22 Thickness Guide

5.3.2.2 Length of the garment

The length of the garment should be clearly mentioned along with the unit.

- length (inches) :17

5.3.2.3 Wash Care

Wash care should cover the following attributes:

- Machine wash at normal cycles.
- Do not soak for long time.
- Wash dark colors separately.
- Dry light colors under shade.
- Tumble dry low.
- Line dry.
- Medium iron only.
- Do not bleach.

5.3.2.4 Return Policy

Return policy should cover the following attributes:

- Return policy:
- 7 days hassle free

5.3.2.5 Delivery time

The delivery time should be clearly defined. The customer should know, in how many days the garment will be delivered.

Metros : 3-5 working days.

Other cities : 5-7 working days.

Areas serviceable only by speed post : 15 working days.

5.3.2.6 View of the garment

View or image of the garment helps in visually understand the garment. There should be five to six views to understand the garment well. The view can include- front view, Back view, Side view, Zoomed view, zoomed Fabric view. Five Views of the garment along with Zoom option is shown in figure5.23.

Figure 5.23 Views of the garments to be shown for a garment

5.3.3 Use of video technology

The e-commerce players need to offer a richer experience and also assist in wearing a certain outfit. It further needs to add value by connecting the garment with the occasion. The video could also provide added advantage of helping the customer to take care of the garment so that it can be worn again without compromising on its sheen after several washes.

The special details of the merchandise have to be communicated to the customer which is inherently difficult for them to gauge from a static picture and help them overcome the lack of touch and feel.

Video of the garment provides a greater conceptualization of the overall garment. It gives answers to questions like: How the garment will drape? The unique selling point of the garment, its creation and how it can be worn? The video link can be included on the description page as shown in figure 5.24.

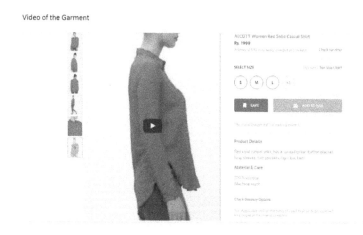

Figure 5.24 The video of the garment can be shown on the description page.

These videos should tell a story behind the garment's stitching and craftsmanship, or showcase how it should be worn. The power of visual merchandising and storytelling that comes out together in the video when a designer explains the craft and technique or his point of view in a compelling way. The audio narrative could also include the key features of touch and feel of the garment thereby resolving the questions that the buyer may have in mind. By integrating the video powerfully into the shopping and brand experience a real differentiated online shopping experience to engage the customers can come alive.

A video has been shot with the actual garment created for the research. The video shows, how the unique selling points of the garment along with the choice of adjustable buttons will be communicated to the customer. The expert is also explaining, how the garment can be stylized for several different occasions. This demonstrates the use of video technology to overcome the problem of communication between the buyer and the seller. The video can be seen with the link **https://youtu.be/GODT_CljmqE** as shown in figure 5.25.

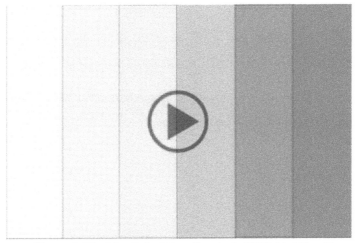

Figure 5.25 video link: https://youtu.be/GODT_CljmqE

In fact, the one-to-one visual engagement between designer and clients for every single piece of apparel can offer a vastly superior experience which will be difficult to replicate in brick-and-mortar retail.

A shot from the video where an expert is describing the garment is shown in figure 5.26.

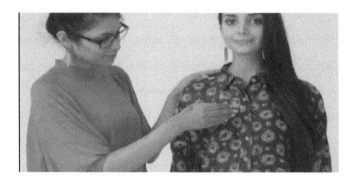

Figure 5.26 A shot from the video made where an expert is describing the garment

Therefore, it is important to exploit the power of visual merchandising on hi-quality display of customer's computer and mobile phone.

The use of video technology also allows for a superior customer experience and overall consumer satisfaction.

CHAPTER 6

CONCLUSIONS AND FUTURE WORK

'Our imagination is the only limit to what we can hope to have in the future.'

Charles F. Kettering

6.1 CONCLUSIONS

In the thesis, it has been addressed how fashion e-commerce companies could make use of advancements in Information Technology to sell fashion apparel more effectively. One of the main contributions of this research work has been the identification of the key areas of attention for fashion e-commerce industry namely Size and fit, Colour and product description.

Fashion e-commerce companies must provide the same services and functions that brick-and-mortar stores provide to meet their customer's needs. Recommendations, including use of advanced Information Technology that could potentially be used by fashion e-commerce industry has been provided.

In particular, it has been proposed that the fashion garment that is sold primarily online must be designed, cut and manufactured differently. A new approach on how the garment's USP could be communicated to the buyer using video so that it helps offset need for touch and feel has been presented. Further the use of PANTONE colors to bring uniformity in presenting colors to the buyers has been recommended.

Finally another contribution is in form of software based virtual fitting room , that the e-commerce companies substitute the experience of physical fitting trial room. An algorithm and the source code in PHP is presented to demonstrate the use of virtual fitting room on a website.

6.2 FUTURE WORK

There is a lot of innovation happening in the apparel e-commerce and in future following advancements in IT hold promise to further improvements.

6.2.1 Video Commerce

Weaving online video into ecommerce sites to enhance the customer web experience is where the action is happening . Video discovery platform, when applied to streaming videos, lets viewers explore the video by touching a point of interest on the screen. This technology opens up a new way for internet users to interact with video content.

Video Shopping, Video Commerce or Video e-Commerce is the practice of using video content to promote, sell and support commercial products or services on the Internet. The video can be downloaded and played or streamed to the viewer. Either way, the video often contains clickable links which can open up a web page or a transaction process. The end goal is to convert a shopper into a customer (Useland, 2014) but conversion is not the only metric as View through Rate (VTR) is a common measurement (Enright, 2014) Some merchants realize additional benefit such as Search Engine Optimization (SEO). A typical video commerce application would involve a video which contains a number of clickable objects so that the viewer can click on any of those objects for further information or to purchase them. However, the clickable object may not always be within the video itself, but part of the Flash or HTML5 player used to play back the video.

There is an Indian company called Charmboard which provides a platform to watch videos of the most popular songs of the movies and let viewers simply touch the image they want to explore, without interrupting the video experience in terms of clothes, accessories, place and the information about the characters and let viewers purchase similar clothes & accessories what their favorite characters were wearing in that particular video. They have also created a technology which lets viewers to watch their favorite TV shows/serials and get similar experience of buying apparel & accessories as shown in the TV show/serial. Here's how it works:

When viewers watch the trailer activated with this technology, they can tap the screen with their finger or click with a mouse/pointing device to interact with a character, a location or discover a product, without intruding on the immersive nature of the content. It draws viewers deeper into the content and extends their engagement after the video has ended.

When the viewer clicks any object in the video, the clicks get saved in the charms. Charm icon contains all the clicks of the user, which can be further explored.

This technology uses advanced algorithms to detect points of interest as they move in real-time on the screen. The viewers can simply touch the image they want to explore, without interrupting the experience. All touches are saved and can be accessed by the viewer anytime on the Internet. Engaged consumers want to interact, explore and shop from their favourite movies or TV serials.

Allowing viewers to touch what interests them in a video opens up a whole new world. The platform offers a video content exploration experience to viewers and in doing so offers brands, content owners and video publishers new engagement opportunity (Business Wire India, 2015). The technology has to pick up and very soon shopping for apparel will be through videos.

6.2.2 HAPTICS

Use of Haptics when shopping via smart phones is suggested as a possible solution of future to communicate texture of the fabric. The sensory features of a smart phone such as vibration and audio feedback could be included to enrich the user experience by recreating important dimensions of human tactile perception such as roughness or friction.

ANNEXURE-I

The correlation between the attributes and their impact where people shifted from online buying to offline buying in the last six months.

The following attributes were significant:

Call:

glm(formula = shift_.from_online_to_.offline ~ Rate_offline_touch_feel_fabric + Rate_offline_testing_fit_size + Rate_offline_get_the_product_sametime + returngarment_colorproblem_rest + returngarment_fabricquality_rest + returngarment_productnotsame_rest, family = "binomial", data = ecommerce_data)

Deviance Residuals:

Min	1Q	Median	3Q	Max
-1.0405	-0.5626	-0.4367	-0.3252	2.6444

Coefficients:

	Estimate	Std. Error	z value	Pr($>|z|$)	
(Intercept)	-5.1292	1.2051	-4.256	2.08e-05	***
Rate_offline_touch_feel_fabric	0.2049	0.1548	1.324	0.1856	
Rate_offline_testing_fit_size	0.2900	0.1631	1.778	0.0754	.
Rate_offline_get_the_product_sametime	0.3213	0.1873	1.715	0.0863	.
returngarment_colorproblem_rest	0.7547	0.4385	1.721	0.0852	.
returngarment_fabricquality_rest	0.5387	0.3768	1.430	0.1529	

returngarment_productnotsame_rest   0.5927   0.4849   1.222   0.2216

$concordance

[1] 0.6052632

$num_concordant

[1] 23

$discordance

[1] 0.3421053

$num_discordant

[1] 13

$tie_rate

[1] 0.05263158

$num_tied

[1] 2

> ###### odds ratio ###########

\>

\>confint(logit) ## CIs using profiled log-likelihood

Waiting for profiling to be done...

	2.5 %	97.5 %
(Intercept)	-7.66296036	-2.9039226
Rate_offline_touch_feel_fabric	-0.09045466	0.5205357
Rate_offline_testing_fit_size	-0.02060670	0.6225179
Rate_offline_get_the_product_sametime	-0.04158861	0.6960392
returngarment_colorproblem_rest	-0.14768658	1.5883205
returngarment_fabricquality_rest	-0.20991940	1.2770574
returngarment_productnotsame_rest	-0.41669101	1.5106574

exp(coef(logit)) ## odds ratios only

(Intercept)	0.005921002
Rate_offline_touch_feel_fabric	1.227369354
Rate_offline_testing_fit_size	1.336481895
Rate_offline_get_the_product_sametime	1.378876074
returngarment_colorproblem_rest	2.127054121
returngarment_fabricquality_rest	1.713777529
returngarment_productnotsame_rest	1.80879

ANNEXURE-II

The correlation between the attributes and their impact where people shifted from offline to online shopping of apparel.

Call:

glm(formula = lastsixmonthsoffline_to_online ~ +Rate_online_home_delivery + Rate_online_consider_price + Shop_preferenceol_discount_rest + video_explaining_designer_point_of_viewyes_no + Size_chart_reliableyes_no,

  family = "binomial", data = ecommerce_data)

Deviance Residuals:

  Min   1Q   Median   3Q   Max
  -1.1391 -0.7050 -0.5707 -0.3858 2.3276

Coefficients:

	Estimate	Std. Error	z value	Pr(>|z|)	
(Intercept)	-4.0932	0.7573	-5.405	6.49e-08	***
Rate_online_home_delivery	0.2335	0.1187	1.968	0.0491	*
Rate_online_consider_price	0.2773	0.1182	2.346	0.0190	*
Shop_preferenceol_discount_rest	0.3429	0.3156	1.087	0.2772	
video_explaining_designer_point_of_viewyes_no	0.6300	0.4693	1.342	0.1795	
Size_chart_reliableyes_no	0.4754	0.3152	1.508	0.1315	

Signif. codes: 0 '***' 0.001 '**' 0.01 '*' 0.05 '.' 0.1 ' ' 1

Call:

$concordance

[1] 0.6610169

$num_concordant

[1] 39

$discordance

[1] 0.2881356

$num_discordant

[1] 17

$tie_rate

[1] 0.05084746

odds ratio

>

>confint(logit) ## CIs using profiled log-likelihood

Waiting for profiling to be done...

	2.5 %	97.5 %
(Intercept)	-5.657588931	-2.6764742
Rate_online_home_delivery	0.004179768	0.4710497
Rate_online_consider_price	0.049400814	0.5145372
Shop_preferenceol_discount_rest	-0.265142239	0.9777062
video_explaining_designer_point_of_view yes_no	-0.225994567	1.6446751
Size_chart_reliable yes_no	-0.131220235	1.1101589

>exp(coef(logit)) ## odds ratios only

(Intercept)	0.01668635
Rate_online_home_delivery	1.26306356
Rate_online_consider_price	1.31952464
Shop_preferenceol_discount_rest	1.40906527
video_explaining_designer_point_of_viewyes_no	1.87758909
Size_chart_reliableyes_no	1.60873705

ANNEXURE-III

The correlation between the attributes and their impact on people, who shop online

Call:

glm(formula = RecentOnline_rest ~ Rate_online_home_delivery + video_explaining_designer_point_of_viewyes_no + Size_chart_reliableyes_no + virtualversusman, family = "binomial", data = ecommerce_data)

Deviance Residuals:

Min	1Q	Median	3Q	Max
-1.7904	-1.3051	0.7962	0.9748	1.4339

Coefficients:

	Estimate	Std. Error	z value	Pr($>$$|z|$)	
(Intercept)	-0.98086	0.45782	-2.142	0.0322	*
Rate_online_home_delivery	0.19781	0.09646	2.051	0.0403	*
video_explaining_designer_point_of_viewyes_no	0.48896	0.31415	1.556	0.1196	
Size_chart_reliableyes_no	0.48918	0.25016	1.955	0.0505	.
virtualversusman	0.39153	0.25745	1.521	0.1283	

Signif. codes: 0 '***' 0.001 '**' 0.01 '*' 0.05 '.' 0.1 ' ' 1

ANNEXURE 4

SOURCE CODE: 1

Source code for the product

```html
<!DOCTYPE html><html lang="en">
<head>
<meta http-equiv="Content-Type" content="text/html; charset=UTF-8">
<meta name="viewport" content="width=device-width">
<meta http-equiv="X-UA-Compatible" content="IE=edge">
<meta name="msapplication-tap-highlight" content="no">
<meta name="apple-mobile-web-app-capable" content="yes">
<meta name="apple-mobile-web-app-title" content="VANHEUSEN"/>
<meta name="application-name" content="VANHEUSEN"/>
<meta name="msapplication-config" content="https://assets.abfrlcdn.com/img/app/favicon/vh/browserconfig.xml"/>
<meta name="theme-color" content="#000000"/>
<title>Van Heusen Shirts, Van Heusen Blue Shirt for Men at Vanheusenindia.com</title>
```

```html
<meta name="description" content="Buy Van Heusen Shirts online at vanheusenindia.com - Shop Online for Van Heusen Van Heusen Blue Shirt for Men at Best Price with Free Shipping & 30 days Return Policy.">

<meta name="keywords" content="">

<meta itemprop="name" content="">

<meta itemprop="description" content="Buy Van Heusen Shirts online at vanheusenindia.com - Shop Online for Van Heusen Van Heusen Blue Shirt for Men at Best Price with Free Shipping & 30 days Return Policy.">

<meta itemprop="image" content="https://assets.abfrlcdn.com/img/app/product/2/207096-638641-large.jpg">

<meta name="twitter:card" content="summary"/>

<meta name="twitter:site" content="@vanheusen ">

<meta name="twitter:title" content="Van Heusen Shirts, Van Heusen Blue Shirt for Men at Vanheusenindia.com">

<meta name="twitter:description" content="Buy Van Heusen Shirts online at vanheusenindia.com - Shop Online for Van Heusen Van Heusen Blue Shirt for Men at Best Price with Free Shipping & 30 days Return Policy.">

<meta name="twitter:creator" content="@vanheusen">

<meta name="twitter:image:src" content="https://assets.abfrlcdn.com/img/app/product/2/207096-638641-large.jpg">
```

```html
<meta name="twitter:url" content="https://www.vanheusenindia.com/van-heusen-blue-shirt-207096.html"/>

<meta property="og:title" content="Van Heusen Shirts, Van Heusen Blue Shirt for Men at Vanheusenindia.com "/>

<meta property="og:description" content="Buy Van Heusen Shirts online at vanheusenindia.com - Shop Online for Van Heusen Van Heusen Blue Shirt for Men at Best Price with Free Shipping & 30 days Return Policy."/>

<meta property="og:site_name" content=""/>

<meta property="og:image" content="https://assets.abfrlcdn.com/img/app/product/2/207096-638641-large.jpg"/>

<meta property="og:url" content="https://www.vanheusenindia.com/van-heusen-blue-shirt-207096.html"/>

<meta property="fb:app_id" content="1782365025315603"/>

<!--[if lte IE 9]><link exclude href="https://assets.abfrlcdn.com/css/app/comb/bflyte_desktop/production/internet_explorer.css" rel="stylesheet" type="text/css"><![endif]-->

<link rel="apple-touch-icon" sizes="180x180" href="https://assets.abfrlcdn.com/img/app/favicon/vh/withBg/favicon-180.png"/>
```

```html
<link rel="manifest" href="https://assets.abfrlcdn.com/img/app/favicon/vh/manifest.json"/>
<link rel="mask-icon" href="https://assets.abfrlcdn.com/img/app/favicon/vh/safari-pinned-tab.svg" color="#5bbad5">
<link href="https://assets.abfrlcdn.com/css/app/comb/bflyte_desktop/production/vh_common.css" rel="stylesheet" type="text/css">
<link href="https://assets.abfrlcdn.com/css/app/comb/bflyte_desktop/production/product.css" rel="stylesheet" type="text/css" property="stylesheet"/>
<link itemprop="availability" href="http://schema.org/InStock"/>
</head>
<body class="vanheusenindia">
<div class="menu_overlay"></div>
<div class="container-fluid header-block vh-header-block">
<div class="row clearfix">
</div>
</div>
<section class="body_wrapper">
```

```html
<div class="container container_body_inner scroll_head_top" itemscope itemtype="http://schema.org/Product">

<input type="hidden" value="207096" id="sleProductID"/>

<input type="hidden" value="" id="sleProductAttributeID"/>

<input type="hidden" value="" id="sleStoreProductAttributeID"/>

<input type="hidden" value="" id="sleStoreCode"/>

<input type="hidden" value="" id="sleStoreEAN"/>

<input type="hidden" value="" id="sleCityId"/>

<input id="wishlistpid" type="hidden" value="0">

<div class="row">

<div class="breadcrumb">

<a title="return to Van Heusen" href="#">Blue Shirt</a>

</div>

<div class="product_image_block">

<div class="row">

<div class="col-lg-6 col-md-6 col-sm-6 col-xs-6">

<div class="product_tabs_wrap">

<div class="product-thumb-view">

<ul class="product_tabs_menu clearfix bxslider" id="thumblist">
```

```html
<li>
  <a href="javascript:void(0);" class="naveImage zoomThumbActive">
    <img title="Van Heusen Blue Shirt" alt="Van Heusen Blue Shirt" src="https://assets.abfrlcdn.com/img/app/others/img1x1.png" data-src="https://assets.abfrlcdn.com/img/app/product/2/207096-638641-small.jpg">
  </a>
</li>
<li>
  <a href="javascript:void(0);" class="naveImage zoomThumbActive">
    <img title="Van Heusen Blue Shirt" alt="Van Heusen Blue Shirt" src="https://assets.abfrlcdn.com/img/app/others/img1x1.png" data-src="https://assets.abfrlcdn.com/img/app/product/2/207096-638639-small.jpg">
  </a>
</li>
<li>
  <a href="javascript:void(0);" class="naveImage zoomThumbActive">
    <img title="Van Heusen Blue Shirt" alt="Van Heusen Blue Shirt" src="https://assets.abfrlcdn.com/img/app/others/img1x1.png" data-src="https://assets.abfrlcdn.com/img/app/product/2/207096-638644-small.jpg">
```

```html
            </a>

        </li>

        <li>

            <a href="javascript:void(0);" class="naveImage zoomThumbActive">

                <img title="Van Heusen Blue Shirt" alt="Van Heusen Blue Shirt" src="https://assets.abfrlcdn.com/img/app/others/img1x1.png" data-src="https://assets.abfrlcdn.com/img/app/product/2/207096-638640-small.jpg">

            </a>

        </li>

        <li>

            <a href="javascript:void(0);" class="naveImage zoomThumbActive">

                <img title="Van Heusen Blue Shirt" alt="Van Heusen Blue Shirt" src="https://assets.abfrlcdn.com/img/app/others/img1x1.png" data-src="https://assets.abfrlcdn.com/img/app/product/2/207096-638642-small.jpg">

            </a>

        </li>

    </ul>

    <div class="outside">

        <div id="slider-prev"></div> <div id="slider-next"></div>
```

```html
</div>

</div>

<div class="product_tabs_content">

<div class="product-wishlist-cont clearfix">

<a href="javascript:void(0);" class="product-wishlist-subcont clearfix ga-tracking">

<div class="pull-left bordered-heart"><img src="https://assets.abfrlcdn.com/img/app/others/img1x1.png" data-src="https://assets.abfrlcdn.com/img/app/others/heart_bordered.png" alt="saved items heart"/></div>

</a>

<div class="clearfix product-wishlist-aftersavecont">

<div class="pull-left product-savd-item-content"><div class="heart orange-heart pull-left"></div> <span class="pull-left font-12 gray-light-color product-wishlist-savedcont"></span></div>

</div>

</div>

<div class="clearfix" id="product_image">

<a href="javascript:void(0);" class="" rel="alternate" title="">

<img id="product_thick_block" src="https://assets.abfrlcdn.com/img/app/product/2/207096-638641-
```

```html
large.jpg" title="Van Heusen Blue Shirt" alt="Van Heusen Blue Shirt" class="img-responsive"/>

<span class="default_magnifier"><i class="tr tr-search-plus"></i></span>

</a>

</div>

</div>

</div>

</div>

<div class="col-lg-6 col-sm-6 col-xs-6">

<div class="pull-right">

<div style="width:100px;">

<div class="coloredSquare" style="background-color: #BAD1E1;width:100px;height:100px;"></div>

<div style="padding: 10px;border:1px solid #eee;font-size:10px;">PANTONE 13-4200 TPX Omphalodes</div>

</div>

</div>

<div class="product_main_info">
```

```html
<h2 itemprop="name"> Blue Shirt </h2>

<span class="font-11 gray-light-color" style="padding:0 0 15px 0;
display:block;">STYLE CODE : VHSF1M76881</span>

<div class="instore-size select_size clearfix" style="display:none;">

<div class="row">

<div class="col-lg-3 col-sm-3 col-md-3 col-xs-3 no_paddingright">

<div class="product-label font-12 gray-light-color font-opensans-
light">In-store Size - </div>

</div>

<div class="col-lg-9 col-sm-9 col-md-9 col-xs-9 no_paddingleft">

<div class="clearfix">

<div class="size_loading text-center"><span class="loader_icon"><img
src="https://assets.abfrlcdn.com/img/app/others/img1x1.png" data-
src="https://assets.abfrlcdn.com/img/app/others/loader_icon_6.gif"
alt=""></span></div>

<ul class="pull-left"></ul></div>

<span id="divLastFewStock" class="divLastFewStock"></span>

</div>

</div>

</div>

<div class="online-size select_size clearfix">
```

```html
<div class="row">
<div class="col-lg-3 col-sm-3 col-md-3 col-xs-3 no_paddingright">
<div class="product-label font-12 gray-light-color font-opensans-light">Online Size - </div>
</div>
<div class="col-lg-3 col-sm-3 col-md-3 col-xs-3 no_paddingleft">
<div class="clearfix">
<div class="size_loading text-center"><span class="loader_icon"><img src="https://assets.abfrlcdn.com/img/app/others/img1x1.png" data-src="https://assets.abfrlcdn.com/img/app/others/loader_icon_6.gif" alt=""></span></div>
<ul class="pull-left"></ul>
</div>
<span id="divLastFewStock" class="divLastFewStock"></span>
</div>
</div>
</div>
<div style="text-align: center; padding: 5px; border: 1px dashed red; color: #ff0000; display: none; margin-bottom:20px;width:30%;" id="noStock"> Out of Stock! </div>
<div class="check-availability select_size">
```

```html
<div class="row">
    <div class="col-lg-8 col-sm-8 col-md-8 col-xs-8">
    </div>
    <div class="col-lg-3 col-sm-3 col-md-3 col-xs-3 pull-right">
    </div>
</div>
</div>
<a style="cursor:pointer;display: inline-block;" href='/fresh11/get_measurements.php'><input type="button" value="Virtual Fitting Room" data-loading-text="Loading..." class="orange-btn-lg font-18 color-white orange-bg col-lg-12 col-md-12 col-sm-12 col-xs-12"/></a>
<div class="modal fade" id="myModal" tabindex="-1" role="dialog" aria-labelledby="myModalLabel">
    <div class="modal-dialog" role="document">
        <div class="modal-content">
            <div class="modal-body" id="fitrratiDiv"></div>
        </div>
    </div>
</div>
<div class="rec clearfix"></div>
```

```html
<div class="view_fit_details clearfix"></div>
<div class="content_block clearfix">
<div class="pattern_divider"></div>
<div class="row shipping_detail_div">
<div class="col-lg-6 col-sm-6 col-xs-6" itemprop="offers" itemscope="" itemtype="http://schema.org/Offer">
<div class="price_loading text-center"><span class="loader_icon"><img src="https://assets.abfrlcdn.com/img/app/others/img1x1.png" data-src="https://assets.abfrlcdn.com/img/app/others/loader_icon_6.gif" alt=""></span></div>
<span itemprop="priceCurrency" class="hide" content="INR"> Rs </span>
<span itemprop="price" content="3499.00"></span>
<div class="price_block" id="divProductPrice"></div>
</div>
<div class="col-lg-6 col-sm-6 col-xs-6">
<div class="ship_block">
<ul>
<li>
```

```html
<a target="_blank" title=""
href="https://www.vanheusenindia.com/content/returns-exchange-policy-
7" class="return">30 days <b>Returns*</b></a>

</li>

<li class="liShipping">

<a title="" target="_blank"
href="https://www.vanheusenindia.com/content/shipping-policy-1"
class="shipping">All India <b>FREE</b> Shipping</a>

</li>

</ul>

</div>

</div>

</div>

<div class="pattern_divider"></div>

</div>

<div class="button_block">

<div class="row">

<div class="col-lg-6 col-sm-6 col-xs-6">

<div class="button_block_inner">

<div id="divAddToBag" class="arrow_box"
style="display:none;">Please select size</div>
```

```html
<input type="button" value="Add to Cart" data-loading-text="Loading..." class="orange-btn-lg font-18 color-white orange-bg col-lg-12 col-md-12 col-sm-12 col-xs-12" id="btnAddToBag"/>

</div>

</div>

<div class="col-lg-6 col-sm-6 col-xs-6">

<div class="button_block_inner">

</div>

</div>

</div>

</div>

<div class="cod-delivery">

<div class="row">

<div class="col-lg-12 col-md-12 col-sm-12 col-xs-12">

<div class="col-lg-6 col-md-6 col-sm-6 col-xs-6 no-gutter">

<div class="ship_block" style="display:none;">

<ul>

<li>

<p class="delivery" href="#" target="_blank">Delivery within <b>3-7 Days</b></p>
```

```html
</li>

<li>

<p class="cod" href="#" target="_blank"><b>COD</b> Available</p>

</li>

</ul>

</div>

</div>

</div>

</div>

</div>

<div class="pincode_section">

<div class="row">

<div class="col-lg-12 col-md-12 col-sm-12 col-xs-12">

<div class="input-group pincode_section_inner">

<div class="row">

<div class="col-lg-10 col-sm-10 col-xs-10">

<input type="text" class="form-control" id="slePincode" maxlength="6" placeholder="Enter 6 digit PIN code" aria-describedby="basic-addon2" style="width:44%; padding:5px 10px;"/>
```

```html
<input type="button" value="Check Estimated Delivery" class="orange-btn-sm gray-dark-bg color-white font-12" id="btnValidatePincode" onclick="TRENDIN.ValidatePincode($('#slePincode').val());" style="width:56%;"/>

</div>

<div class="delvry-error pull-left " id="divPincodeValidationErrorResult">

</div>

<div class="delvry-success pull-left" id="divPincodeValidationSuccessResult">

</div>

</div>

</div>

</div>

</div>

</div>

<div class="share_section dropdown">

<a class="dropdown-toggle font-14" data-toggle="dropdown" href="#">

<i class="tr tr-share pull-left"></i>

<span class="share-title">Share</span>

</a>
```

```html
<ul class="dropdown-menu mega-dropdown-menu">

<li>

<a
onClick="window.open('https://www.facebook.com/sharer.php?u=www.v
anheusenindia.com/product/van-heusen-blue-shirt-
207096.html','sharer','status=0,width=580,height=325');"
href="javascript: void(0)">

<img
src="https://assets.abfrlcdn.com/img/app/others/facebook_share.png"
alt="facebook-share" title="facebook-share"/>

<p>Facebook</p>

</a>

</li>

<li>

<a class="twitter customer share"
href="http://twitter.com/share?url=https://www.vanheusenindia.com/prod
uct/van-heusen-blue-shirt-207096.html&amp;text=I ♥ this product on Van
Heusen India" target="_blank">

<img src="https://assets.abfrlcdn.com/img/app/others/twitter_share.png"
alt="twitter-share" title="twitter-share"/>

<p>Twitter</p>

</a>
```

```html
</li>

</ul>

</div>

<div class="share-touch-view">

<p class="pull-left">Share on :</p>

<a onClick="window.open('https://www.facebook.com/sharer.php?u=www.vanheusenindia.com/product/van-heusen-blue-shirt-207096.html','sharer','status=0,width=580,height=325');" href="javascript: void(0)" class="pull-left">

<img src="https://assets.abfrlcdn.com/img/app/others/facebook_share.png" alt="facebook-share" title="facebook-share"/>

</a>

<a class="twitter customer share" href="http://twitter.com/share?url=https://www.vanheusenindia.com/product/van-heusen-blue-shirt-207096.html&amp;text=I ♥ this product on Van Heusen India" target="_blank" class="pull-left">

<img src="https://assets.abfrlcdn.com/img/app/others/twitter_share.png" alt="twitter-share" title="twitter-share"/>

</a>

</div>
```

```html
        </div>

    </div>

<div class="clearfix"></div>

<div class="product_detail_block">

<div class="row">

<div class="col-lg-6 col-sm-6 col-xs-6">

<div class="info_div product_desc_lhs">

<h3 class="active" data-toggle="collapse" data-target="#prod_desc">Product Description <i class="tr tr-angle-up"></i></h3>

<div class="content collapse in" id="prod_desc" itemprop="description">

<p> For a distinctly stylish corporate look, don this blue/PANTONE 13-4200 TPX Omphalodes shirt. Spun from cotton, this design is comfortable to wear from 9 to 5 and beyond. Wear this full sleeve piece with black trousers and Oxfords for an impeccable ensemble. </p>

</div>

</div>

<div class="info_div product_desc_lhs">
```

```html
<h3 class="active" data-toggle="collapse" data-target="#prod_feature">Product Features <i class="tr tr-angle-up"></i></h3>

<div class="content collapse in" id="prod_feature">

<span class="strong">Brand</span> : Van Heusen<br>

<span class="strong">Cuffs</span> : Regular Cuff<br>

<span class="strong">Collar</span> : Regular Collar<br>

<span class="strong">Material</span> : 100% Cotton<br>

<span class="strong">Sleeves</span> : Full Sleeves<br>

<span class="strong">Subbrand</span> : Van Heusen<br>

<span class="strong">Fit</span> : Comfort Fit<br>

<span class="strong">Pattern</span> : Solid<br>

<span class="strong">Occasion</span> : Formal<br>

<span class="strong">Color</span> : blue/PANTONE 13-4200 TPX Omphalodes<br>

</div>

</div>

</div>

<div id="infinite_analytics_div" class="col-lg-6 col-sm-6 col-xs-6"></div>
```

```
<div id="infinite_analytics_widget" class="col-lg-6 col-sm-6 col-xs-
6"></div>

</div>

</div>

<div class="trendIn_message">

<div class="pattern_divider"></div>

</div>

<div class="product_user_view">

<div class="row">

<div class="col-lg-6 col-md-6 col-sm-6 col-xs-6">

<div class="recent_view_block">

</div>

</div>

<div class="col-lg-6 col-md-6 col-sm-6 col-xs-6">

<div class="cross_buy_block">

</div>

</div>

</div>

</div>
```

```html
</div>

<div class="similar_product_view"></div>

<div class="sizeguide_popup_container">

<div class="modal fade" id="myModal_sizeguide" tabindex="-1" role="dialog" aria-labelledby="myModalLabel" aria-hidden="true" data-backdrop="static" data-keyboard="false">

<div class="modal-dialog modal-lg">

<div class="modal-content">

<div class="modal-header">

<button type="button" class="close" data-dismiss="modal" aria-label="Close"><span aria-hidden="true">&times;</span></button>

<h4 class="modal-title" id="myModalLabel">Size Guide</h4>

</div>

<div class="modal-body">

<div class="size_guide_wrap">

<div class="size_guide_head clearfix">

<h3 class="pull-left">

Van Heusen Blue Shirt     </h3>

<div class="vanheusen_men_sub pull-right"><img src="https://assets.abfrlcdn.com/img/app/brand_sub/vanheusen_men_sub.png" alt=""/></div>
```

```html
<div class="pull-right"></div>

</div>

<div class="row sizeguide_data">

</div>

</div>

</div>

</div>

</div>

</div>

</div>

</section>

<div class="modal fade try-atstore-view" tabindex="-1" role="dialog" aria-labelledby="myModalLabel" data-backdrop="static" id="TryAtStoreData">

<div class="selectsize-dialog modal-dialog" style="display:none">

<div class="selectsize-content">

<div class="selectsize-header" style="border-bottom:none !important;">

<h5 class="modal-title font-opensans-sb" id="myModalLabel">SELECT SIZE</h5>

</div>
```

```html
<div class="row selectsize-body">

<ul class="col-lg-11 col-sm-11 col-md-11 col-xs-11 col-lg-offset-1 col-md-offset-1 tryatstore-selectsize">

</ul>

</div>

<div class="row selectsize-footer padding-zero">

<a href="#1" data-dismiss="modal" aria-label="Close" class="col-lg-3 col-sm-3 col-md-3 col-xs-3 pull-right text-center font-14 gray-color padding-zero">CANCEL</a>

<a href="#" class="col-lg-2 col-sm-2 col-md-2 col-xs-2 pull-right text-center font-14 orange-color padding-zero triger-tryatstore">OK</a>

</div>

</div>

</div>

<div class="modal-dialog tryatstore-dialog" role="document">

<div class="modal-content">

<div class="modal-header" style="border-bottom:none !important;">

<a href="#" class="close font-16 tryatstore-cancel" data-dismiss="modal" aria-label="Close">CLOSE</a>

<h4 class="modal-title" id="myModalLabel">SELECT SIZE AND PREFERRED STORE</h4>
```

```html
        </div>
        <div class="modal-body">
            <div class="form-row store-code-view">
                <label class="product-label font-14 gray-color font-opensans-light pull-left">Store:</label>
                <input type="text" class="col-md-5 col-sm-5 col-xs-5 store-search" placeholder="Enter your locality or city" name="" id="sleSearchStores"/>
                <input type="hidden" class="searchLocality" value="">
                <div id="cityAvailable" class="stylecode-autosuggest" style="display:block;">
                </div>
                <div class="clearfix"></div>
            </div>
            <div class="form-row availablesizes">
                <label class="product-label font-14 gray-color font-opensans-light pull-left">Size:</label>
                <ul class="col-lg-9 col-sm-9 col-md-9 col-xs-9 tryatstore_sizechart">
                </ul>
                <div class="clearfix"></div>
            </div>
```

```html
<div class="alert-message error-view" style="display:none;">

<span class="font-20 gray-dark-color"></span>

<div class="clearfix"></div>

<span class="font-14 gray-dark-color"></span>

</div>

<div class="alert-message warning-view" style="display:none;">

<span class="font-20 gray-dark-color">Sorry, the item is not available in the stores near 560046</span>

<div class="clearfix"></div>

<span class="font-14 gray-dark-color">You may pick-up items from following stores in Banglore or get the items delivered at your desired address</span>

</div>

<div class="tryatstore-address-list row">

<div class="adress-error">

<span class="adress-error-msg font-18">Please Select Nearby Store address near to you</span>

</div>

<div class="tryatstore-addres">

<h4 class="gray-light-color font-18 font-catamaran-regular">Select Nearby Store : </h4>
```

```html
<div id="TryAtStoreSearchlist" class="carousel slide" data-ride="carousel" data-interval="false">
<div class="carousel-inner" role="listbox">
</div>
<a class="left carousel-control" href="#TryAtStoreSearchlist" role="button" data-slide="prev">
<span class="glyphicon glyphicon-chevron-left" aria-hidden="true">&#x276c;</span>
<span class="sr-only">Previous</span>
</a>
<a class="right carousel-control" href="#TryAtStoreSearchlist" role="button" data-slide="next">
<span class="glyphicon glyphicon-chevron-right" aria-hidden="true">&#x276d;</span>
<span class="sr-only">Next</span>
</a>
</div>
</div>
</div>
<div class="modal-footer">
```

```html
<a href="#1" data-dismiss="modal" aria-label="Close" class="orange-btn-md gray-color-bg color-white col-lg-4 col-sm-4 col-xs-4 pull-right text-center font-16 tryatstore-cancel">CANCEL</a>

<a href="#" class="orange-btn-md orange-bg color-white col-lg-4 col-sm-4 col-xs-4 pull-right text-center font-16 triger-confirm">CONFIRM</a>

</div>

</div>

</div>

</div>

<div class="modal-dialog confirm-dialog address-confirm-view" role="document" style="display:none;">

<div class="modal-content confirm-content">

<div class="modal-header" style="border-bottom:none !important;">

<a href="#" class="close font-16 tryatstore-cancel" data-dismiss="modal" aria-label="Close">CLOSE</a>

<h4 class="modal-title" id="myModalLabel">SELECT SIZE AND PREFFERED STORE</h4>

</div>

<div class="confirm-header">
```

```html
<p class="modal-title font-opensans-sb font-20" id="myModalLabel">Van Heusen Blue Shirt( Size : <span id="size-assign-id"></span>)<br/>is added to your Try&Buy Bag.</p>

<p class="font-15 font-opensans-light">You can continue to select more products to try at your selected store</p>

</div>

<div class="confirm-body">

<div class="tryatstore-confirm-addres-col col-md-6 col-sm-6 col-xs-6">

<div class="tryatstore-addres-col">

</div>

<div class="address-change-view">

<a href="#" class="font-12 edit-address pull-left">CHANGE</a>

</div>

</div>

<input type="hidden" value="https://www.vanheusenindia.com/category/collections-77" id="redirectionUrl"/>

<input type="hidden" value="" id="selectedAreaIdProduct"/>

<a onclick="callBackToCategoryPage()" href="javascript:void(0);" class="tryatstore-confirm-addres-col-side orange-color font-15 font-opensans-light pull-left" style="text-transfrom:uppercase;">
```

Shop more products <br> from this store

<span class="arrow font-opensans-light">❭</span>

</a>

<div class="clearfix"></div>

<div class="confirm-dialog-proceed font-15 font-opensans-light">

or proceed to your Try&Buy bag to schedule trial for the items

</div>

<div class="clearfix"></div>

<a onclick="calltrystore()" href="javascript:void(0)" class="confirm-dialog-bag orange-color font-20">TRY&BUY BAG</a>

</div>

<div class="modal-footer">

<a href="#1" data-dismiss="modal" aria-label="Close" class="col-lg-2 col-sm-2 col-md-2 col-xs-2 pull-right text-center font-14 gray-color">CANCEL</a>

<a href="#3" data-dismiss="modal" class="col-lg-1 col-sm-1 col-md-1 col-xs-1 pull-right text-center font-14 orange-color">OK</a>

<div class="clearfix"></div>

</div>

</div>

```html
                </div>

            </div>




    <div class="footer_buttons">
        <a class="top load_click_ie" href="javascript:void(0);"></a>
    </div>
    <div class="login_pop_wrap vanheusenindia-authentication">
        <div class="modal fade" id="divLoginRegister">
            <div class="modal-dialog">
                <button type="button" class="close" data-dismiss="modal" aria-label="Close">X CLOSE</button>
                <div class="modal-content">
                    <div class="modal-header">
                        <div class="row margin-zero">
                            <div class="col-lg-2 col-md-2 col-sm-2 col-xs-2 tabheader font-16 gray-color active register-tab cursor-pointer">Register</div>
                            <div class="col-lg-2 col-md-2 col-sm-2 col-xs-2 tabheader font-16 gray-color login-tab cursor-pointer">Login</div>
```

```html
<div class="col-lg-5 col-md-5 col-sm-5 col-xs-5 pull-right peoplebrand-logo padding-zero">

<div></div><div></div><div></div><div></div><div></div><div></div><div></div>

</div>

</div>

</div>

<div class="modal-body">

<div class="login_existing">

<div class="row">

<div class="col-lg-6 col-md-6 col-sm-6 col-xs-6">

<h3>Login with your registered Mobile number or Email</h3>

<form id="frmLoginPopupForm" autocomplete="on" method="POST">

<div class="form-group">

<input type="text" class="inputMaterial form-control" id="sleCustomerMobNo" maxlength="" required>

<label class="gray-light-color font-14" for="sleCustomerMobNo">Mobile Number or Email<span>*</span></label>

<span class="err_msg">Please enter mobile number or email</span>

</div>
```

```html
<div class="form-group">

<input type="password" class="inputMaterial form-control" id="sleCustomerPassword" maxlength="32" required>

<a href="javascript:void(0);" class="font-10 gray-dark-color login-show-password">SHOW</a>

<label class="gray-light-color font-14" for="sleCustomerPassword">Password<span>*</span></label>

<span class="err_msg">Please enter password</span>

</div>

<a class="forgot_password pull-left" id="forgot_password" href="javascript:void(0);">Forgot your Password?</a>

<button type="button" class="brand-bg brand-btn color-white font-14" id="btnCustomerLogin" data-loading-text="Loading...">Login</button>

</form>

</div>

<div class="col-lg-5 col-md-5 col-sm-5 col-xs-5 pull-right" style="display:none;">

<h3>Or use your social accounts to login</h3>

<a class="signin_goog" href="https://www.vanheusenindia.com/auth/login/google">

<span><i class="tr tr-google-plus"></i></span>
```

```html
<span>Sign in with Google</span>

</a>

<a class="signin_fb"
href="https://www.vanheusenindia.com/auth/login/facebook">

<span><i class="tr tr-facebook"></i></span>

<span>Sign in with Facebook</span>

</a>

</div>

</div>

<div class="modal-footer">

</div>

</div>

<div class="forgot_password_view">

<div class="forgot_password_block">

<div class="error_msg"></div>

<div class="forgot_password_form_div" id="forgotpasswordformdiv">

<h3><b>Forgot Password</b></h3>

<form action="https://www.vanheusenindia.com/login/forgotPassword"
method="post" accept-charset="utf-8" id="form_forgot_password"
autocomplete="on">
```

```html
<div class="form-group forgotmob">
<input type="text" name="forgotmob" class="inputMaterial form-control" id="forgotmob" maxlength="" required>
<label class="gray-light-color font-14" for="forgotmob">Enter mobile number or email<span>*</span></label>
</div>
<button type="submit" class="brand-bg brand-btn color-white pull-left col-md-9" data-loading-text="Loading...">Forgot My Password</button>
<div class="clearfix"></div>
</form>
<form id="form_forgotpassword_otp" autocomplete="off">
<p style="margin:10px 0 20px 0;">Reset your password by clicking on the link send to your <b>Email ID</b> OR Enter the <b>6 digit OTP verification number</b> sent to your mobile number</p>
<div class="form-group" style>
<input autocomplete="otp-forgotpassword" type="text" class="inputMaterial form-control" name="otpforgotpassword" id="OTPforgotpassword" minlength="6" maxlength="6" required>
<label class="gray-light-color font-14" for="OTPforgotpassword">OTP<span>*</span></label>
<span class="err_msg"></span>
```

```html
</div>

<div class="clearfix">

<button type="button" id="forgotResendOTP" class="brand-bg brand-btn color-white font-14 pull-left" data-loading-text="Loading...">Resend OTP</button>

<button type="button" id="forgotOTPcheck" class="brand-bg brand-btn color-white font-14 pull-right" data-loading-text="Loading...">APPLY</button>

</div>

</form>

<form id="reset-passcode" autocomplete="off" method="POST">

<div class="form-group" style="margin:10px 0 25px 0">

<input autocomplete="otp-forgotpassword" type="password" class="inputMaterial form-control" name="otpforgotpassword" id="OTPresetnewpassword" required>

<a href="javascript:void(0);" class="font-10 gray-dark-color login-show-password">SHOW</a>

<label class="gray-light-color font-14" for="OTPforgotpassword">New Password<span>*</span></label>

<span class="err_msg"></span>

</div>
```

```html
<div class="form-group" style="margin-bottom:15px">
<input autocomplete="otp-forgotpassword" type="password" class="inputMaterial form-control" name="otpforgotpassword" id="OTPresetconfirmpassword" required>
<a href="javascript:void(0);" class="font-10 gray-dark-color login-show-password">SHOW</a>
<label class="gray-light-color font-14" for="OTPforgotpassword">Confirm Password<span>*</span></label>
<span class="err_msg"></span>
</div>
<div class="clearfix">
<button type="button" id="resetpasswordOTPcheck" class="brand-bg brand-btn color-white font-14 pull-right" data-loading-text="Loading...">Reset Password</button>
</div>
</form>
</div>
</div>
<div class="modal-footer">
</div>
</div>
```

```html
<div class="login_new">
<div class="row">
<div class="col-lg-6 col-md-6 col-sm-6 col-xs-6 register-default">
<h3>Register with us to get latest updates and manage your orders</h3>
<form id="frmRegistration" autocomplete="off" method="POST">
<div class="form-group gender-group">
<span class="err_msg" id="err_gender" style="margin-top: -6px"></span>
<label class="col-md-3 col-sm-3 col-xs-5">
<input type="hidden" name="gender" value="" id="hdnGender1"/>
<input type="radio" name="gender1" role="him" id="rdMaleGender1"/> Mr.
</label>
<label class="col-md-3 col-sm-3 col-xs-5">
<input type="radio" name="gender1" role="her" id="rdFemaleGender1"/> Ms.
</label>
<div class="clearfix"></div>
</div>
<div class="form-group">
```

```html
<input type="text" class="inputMaterial form-control" name="firstname" id="sleFirstName" maxlength="80" required>
<label class="gray-light-color font-14" for="sleFirstName">Name<span>*</span></label>
<span class="err_msg"></span>
</div>
<div class="form-group">
<input type="text" class="inputMaterial form-control" name="mobile" id="sleMobile" maxlength="10" required>
<label class="gray-light-color font-14" for="sleMobile">Mobile Number<span>*</span></label>
<span class="err_msg" id="err_sleMobile"></span>
</div>
<div class="form-group">
<input autocomplete="new-password" type="password" class="inputMaterial form-control" name="password" id="slePassword" minlength="6" maxlength="32" required>
<a href="javascript:void(0);" class="font-10 gray-dark-color login-show-password">SHOW</a>
<label class="gray-light-color font-14" for="slePassword">Password<span>*</span></label>
```

```html
<span class="err_msg"></span>

</div>

<div class="form-group">

<input type="text" class="inputMaterial form-control" name="email" id="sleEmail" maxlength="128" required>

<label class="gray-light-color font-14" for="sleEmail">E-Mail<span>*</span></label>

<span class="err_msg" id="err_sleEmailID"></span>

</div>

<div class="checkbox">

<label>

<input type="checkbox" id="chkTermsConditions" checked="checked" name="tnc"> I agree to the vanheusenindia

<a title="" href="https://www.vanheusenindia.com/content/terms-and-conditions-of-use-3" target="_blank">terms of use</a>

and

<a title="" href="https://www.vanheusenindia.com/content/privacy-policy-13" target="_blank">privacy policy</a>.

<span class="err_msg"></span>

</label>

</div>
```

```html
<div class="clearfix register_btn">

<button type="button" id="register_button1" class="brand-bg brand-btn color-white font-14 pull-right" data-loading-text="Loading...">REGISTER</button>

</div>

</form>

</div>

<div class="col-lg-5 col-md-5 col-sm-5 col-xs-5 pull-right register-default social-login" style="display:none;">

<h3>Or use your social accounts to signup with us</h3>

<a class="signin_goog" href="https://www.vanheusenindia.com/auth/login/google">

<span><i class="tr tr-google-plus"></i></span>

<span>Sign in with Google</span>

</a>

<a class="signin_fb" href="https://www.vanheusenindia.com/auth/login/facebook">

<span><i class="tr tr-facebook"></i></span>

<span>Sign in with Facebook</span>

</a>

</div>
```

```html
<div class="col-lg-8 col-md-8 col-sm-8 col-xs-8 register-otp">

<h3>Enter the 6 digit OTP verification number sent to your mobile number</h3>

<form id="OTPRegistration" autocomplete="off">

<div class="form-group">

<input autocomplete="otp-registration" type="text" class="inputMaterial form-control" name="otpregistration" id="OTPReg" minlength="6" maxlength="6" required>

<label class="gray-light-color font-14" for="OTPReg">OTP<span>*</span></label>

<span class="err_msg"></span>

</div>

<div class="clearfix">

<button type="button" id="registrationResendOTP" class="brand-bg brand-btn color-white font-14 pull-left" data-loading-text="Loading...">Resend OTP</button>

<button type="button" id="registrationOTPcheck" class="brand-bg brand-btn color-white font-14 pull-right" data-loading-text="Loading...">APPLY</button>

</div>

</form>
```

```html
        </div>
    </div>
    <div class="modal-footer">
    </div>
    </div>
    </div>
    </div>
    </div>
    </div>
    </div>
<div class="modal fade trendin-error-alert" id="divTrendinAlert" data-backdrop="static">
    <div class="modal-dialog">
        <div class="modal-content">
            <div class="modal-header" style="border-radius:0px;">
                <button type="button" class="close" data-dismiss="modal" aria-label="Close"><span aria-hidden="true">&times;</span></button>
                <h4 class="modal-title">Van Heusen India</h4>
            </div>
            <div class="modal-body" id="divAlertContent" style="padding:15;">
```

```html
<span class="orange-tri-left"></span>

<p class="text-left pull-left gray-darker-color"> </p>

<a href="javascript:void" class="orange-trs-btn-md orange-color font-16 pull-right" data-dismiss="modal">OK</a>

<div class="clearfix"></div>

</div>

</div>

</div>

</div>

<div class="modal fade" id="divProductQuickView" tabindex="-1" role="dialog" aria-labelledby="myModalLabel" aria-hidden="true" data-backdrop="static">

<div class="modal-dialog modal-lg">

<div class="modal-content">

<div class="modal-body" style="text-align:center;">

<iframe id="ifrmProudctQuickContent" frameborder="0" scrolling="no" width="100%" height="585" src="" allowTransparency="true">

</iframe>

</div>

</div>
```

```html
    </div>

  </div>

<div class="confirm_popup">

<div class="modal fade" id="confirm-delete" tabindex="-1" role="dialog" aria-labelledby="myModalLabel" aria-hidden="true">

<div class="modal-dialog">

<div class="modal-content">

<div class="modal-header">

<button type="button" class="close" data-dismiss="modal" aria-hidden="true">&times;</button>

<h4 class="modal-title">Confirm Pop Up</h4>

</div>

<div class="modal-body">

<p>You are about to delete one track, this procedure is irreversible.</p>

<p>Do you want to proceed?</p>

<p class="debug-url"></p>

</div>

<div class="modal-footer">

<a class="btn btn-danger btn-ok pull-right">Yes</a>
```

```html
<button type="button" class="btn btn-default pull-right" data-dismiss="modal">No</button>

</div>

</div>

</div>

</div>

</div>

<div class="bg_overlay" style="display:none;" id="divGlobalLoader">

<div class="loader_icon"><img src="https://assets.abfrlcdn.com/img/app/others/loader_icon_6.gif" alt="loader_icon" width="40" height="40"></div>

</div>

<div class="track_order_view" style="display:none;">

<div class="modal fade track_order" id="myModal_trackorder" tabindex="-1" role="dialog" aria-labelledby="myModalLabel" aria-hidden="true" data-backdrop="static" data-keyboard="false">

<div class="modal-dialog modal-lg">

<div class="modal-content">

<div class="modal-header">
```

```html
<button type="button" class="close" id="track_popup_close" data-dismiss="modal" aria-label="Close"><span aria-hidden="true">&times;</span></button>

<h4 class="modal-title">Track Order</h4>

</div>

<div class="modal-body">

<div class="row">

<div class="col-lg-7 col-lg-offset-2 col-md-7 col-md-offset-2 col-sm-10 col-sm-offset-1 col-xs-12">

<form class="form-horizontal track_order_form" autocomplete="on">

<div class="form-group">

<div class="error col-sm-offset-3 col-sm-10 col-md-offset-3 col-md-10 col-xs-12" id="divErrors" style="display: none;align:center;color:#FF0000">Order no and mobile number is not matching.</div>

</div>

<div class="form-group">

<label for="sleMobileNumber" class="col-md-3 col-sm-3 col-xs-12 control-label">Mobile Number <span class="astriek">*</span></label>

<div class="col-md-9 col-sm-9 col-xs-12">
```

```html
<input type="text" class="form-control" id="sleMobileNumber" value="" placeholder="Please Enter your mobile number"/>

<span id="validation_email_error" class="has-error" style="display:none;align:center;color:#FF0000">Please enter valid mobile number.</span>

</div>

</div>

<div class="form-group">

<label for="sleOrderNumber" class="col-md-3 col-sm-3 col-xs-12 control-label">Order No <span class="astriek">*</span></label>

<div class="col-md-9 col-sm-9 col-xs-12">

<input type="text" class="form-control" id="sleOrderNumber" placeholder="Order ID"/>

<span id="validation_order_error" class="has-error" style="display:none;align:center;color:#FF0000">Please enter valid order no.</span>

</div>

</div>

<div class="form-group">

<div class="col-sm-offset-3 col-sm-9 col-md-offset-3 col-md-9 col-xs-12">

<div class="pull-right">
```

```html
<input type="button" name="trackorder" id="btnTrackOrder" class="orange-btn-md orange-bg color-white font-14" value="Track Order"/>
<input type="button" class="orange-btn-md orange-bg color-white font-14 login_btn top_header_logged_tracker" value="Login for more"/>
</div>
</div>
</div>
</form>
</div>
</div>
<div class="track_order_modal">
</div>
</div>
</div>
</div>
</div>
</div>
<div class="pixel_data" style="display:none;"></div>
<style type="text/css">
```

```html
.social-login{display:none !important;}

</style>

<div id="fb-root"></div>

<div class="modal fade store-view-modal" id="myMapModal" role="dialog" aria-labelledby="myModalLabel">

<div class="modal-dialog modal-lg">

<div class="modal-content">

<div class="modal-body">

<iframe id="google_map_iframe" src="" width="100%" height="500px"></iframe>

</div>

</div>

</div>

<noscript>

<div style="display:inline;">

<img height="1" width="1" style="border-style:none;" alt="" src="//googleads.g.doubleclick.net/pagead/viewthroughconversion/875926909/?guid=ON&amp;script=0"/>

</div>

</noscript>
```

```html
<script type="text/javascript"
src="https://assets.abfrlcdn.com/js/jquery/jquery.min.js"></script>

<script type="text/javascript">(function(){var
ea=document.createElement('script');ea.type='text/javascript';ea.async=true;ea.src='//d3qm5o86jyjko6.cloudfront.net/rec/expertrec_wwwtrendin.js'
;var
m=document.getElementsByTagName('script')[0];m.parentNode.insertBefore(ea,m)})();var _eaq=_eaq||[];function
expertApi(){if(window.expertrec_true){var
args=Array.prototype.slice.call(arguments);window.ea_apispec[args[0]](args.slice(1,args.length))}else{_eaq.push(arguments);}}</script>

<script
type="text/javascript">window._trackJs={token:'29e04df83ab7410aa4f84be1801cb6ae'};</script>

<script type="text/javascript"
src="https://cdn.trackjs.com/releases/current/tracker.js"></script>

<script type="text/javascript">var ABFRL={};var
strBaseURL="https://www.vanheusenindia.com/";var
strSSLBaseURL="https://www.vanheusenindia.com/";var
strLogoBaseURL="https://www.vanheusenindia.com/";var
isCustomerLoggedIn="0";var strPageName="product";var
intCustomerID="";var intCartID="";window.intROPISCartID=0;var
pageType="product";var strShopName="Van Heusen";var
strShopURI="";var
intShopID="6";window.activityid="DONOTTRACK";var
```

environment="production";var app="";var dblMinShippingCartValue="750";var intCategoryID=";var strCategory=";var strGender=";var intSessionStoreCode="";var intRopisPincode="";var searchParam=intSessionPincode="";var searchType=sessionSearchType="";var searchParam=intSessionCity="";var searchStoreCode=intSessionStoreCode="";var searchLocality="";var intProductID='207096';var strProductName="Van Heusen Blue Shirt";var intSellingPrice=0;var strTitle="";var ab=";var sid=";var affiliateName="";var utmMedium="";var utmCampaign="";var strDeviceType="desktop";var strLoggedinUserMailID="";var strEncodedLoggedinUserMailId="";var intLoggedinUserMobileNumber="";var storeloggedIntemp=0;var strSocialLoginFlashData="";var temp_email=temp_Name=";var objLabels={"shopping_cart":"Cart","try&buy":"Try&Buy","store_locator":"Locate Store","track_order":"Track Order","contact":"Contact","left_pnl_order_history":"ORDER HISTORY","left_pnl_wallet":"CREDITS","left_pnl_info":"ACCOUNT & INFORMATION","left_pnl_tryatstore":"TRY&BUY","left_pnl_wishlist":"Saved Items","left_pnl_addresses":"MY ADDRESSES","left_pnl_changepassword":"CHANGE PASSWORD","left_pnl_logout":"LOGOUT"};var arrShopIds_subBrand=['6'];</script>

<script type="text/javascript">if(document.cookie.indexOf("STORECODE")>-

1){window.dataLayer=window.dataLayer||[];window.dataLayer.push({'tvc_kiosk':'kiosk'});}</script>

<script type="text/javascript">(function(w,d,s,l,i){w[l]=w[l]||[];w[l].push({'gtm.start':new Date().getTime(),event:'gtm.js'});var f=d.getElementsByTagName(s)[0],j=d.createElement(s),dl=l!='dataLayer'?'&l='+l:'';j.async=true;j.src='//www.googletagmanager.com/gtm.js?id='+i+dl;f.parentNode.insertBefore(j,f);})(window,document,'script','dataLayer','GTM-PHLTR6');</script>

<script type="text/javascript">function lzld(){}(function(d,h){"function"===typeof define&&define.amd?define(h):"object"===typeof exports?module.exports=h():d.Blazy=h()})(this,function(){function d(b){if(!document.querySelectorAll){var g=document.createStyleSheet();document.querySelectorAll=function(b,a,e,d,f){f=document.all;a=[];b=b.replace(/\[for\b/gi,"[htmlFor").split(",");for(e=b.length;e--;){g.addRule(b[e],"k:v");for(d=f.length;d--;)f[d].currentStyle.k&&a.push(f[d]);g.removeRule(0)}return a}}m=!0;k=[];e={};a=b||{};a.error=a.error||!1;a.offset=a.offset||100;a.success=a.success||!1;a.selector=a.selector||".b-lazy";a.separator=a.separator||"|";a.container=a.container?document.querySelectorAll(a.container):!1;a.errorClass=a.errorClass||"b-error";a.breakpoints=a.breakpoints||!1;a.successClass=a.successClass||"b-loaded";a.src=r=a.src||"data-src";u=1<window.devicePixelRatio;e.top=0-a.offset;e.left=0-a.offset;f=v(w,25);t=v(x,50);x();n(a.breakpoints,function(b){if(b.width>=wi

ndow.screen.width)return r=b.src,!1});h()}function h(){y(a.selector);m&&(m=!1,a.container&&n(a.container,function(b){p(b,"scroll",f)}),p(window,"resize",t),p(window,"resize",f),p(window,"scroll",f));w()}function w(){for(var b=0;b<l;b++){var g=k[b],c=g.getBoundingClientRect();if(c.right>=e.left&&c.bottom>=e.top&&c.left<=e.right&&c.top<=e.bottom||-1!==(" "+g.className+" ").indexOf(" "+a.successClass+" "))d.prototype.load(g),k.splice(b,1),l--,b--}0===l&&d.prototype.destroy()}function z(b,g){if(g||0<b.offsetWidth&&0<b.offsetHeight){var c=b.getAttribute(r)||b.getAttribute(a.src);if(c){var c=c.split(a.separator),d=c[u&&1<c.length?1:0],c=new Image;n(a.breakpoints,function(a){b.removeAttribute(a.src)});b.removeAttribute(a.src);c.onerror=function(){a.error&&a.error(b,"invalid");b.className=b.className+" "+a.errorClass};c.onload=function(){"img"===b.nodeName.toLowerCase()?b.src=d:b.style.backgroundImage='url("'+d+'")';b.className=b.className+" "+a.successClass;a.success&&a.success(b)};c.src=d}else a.error&&a.error(b,"missing"),b.className=b.className+" "+a.errorClass}}function y(b){b=document.querySelectorAll(b);for(var a=l=b.length;a--;)k.unshift(b[a]);}function x(){e.bottom=(window.innerHeight||document.documentElement.clientHeight)+a.offset;e.right=(window.innerWidth||document.documentElement.clientWidth)+a.offset}function p(b,a,c){b.attachEvent?b.attachEvent&&b.attachEvent("on"+a,c):b.addEventListener(a,c,!1)}function q(b,a,c){b.detachEvent?b.detachEvent&&b.detachEvent("on"+a,c):b.rem

oveEventListener(a,c,!1)}function n(a,d){if(a&&d)for(var c=a.length,e=0;e<c&&!1!==d(a[e],e);e++);}function v(a,d){var c=0;return function(){var e=+new Date;e-c<d||(c=e,a.apply(k,arguments))}}var r,a,e,k,l,u,m,f,t;d.prototype.revalidate=function(){h()};d.prototype.load=function(b,d){-1===(" "+b.className+" ").indexOf(" "+a.successClass+" ")&&z(b,d)};d.prototype.destroy=function(){a.container&&n(a.container,function(a){q(a,"scroll",f)});q(window,"scroll",f);q(window,"resize",f);q(window,"resize",t);l=0;k.length=0;m=!0};return d});</script>

<script type="text/javascript">var genderId='3';</script>

<script type="text/javascript" src="https://assets.abfrlcdn.com/js/app/comb/bflyte_desktop/production/product.js"></script>

<script type="text/javascript" src="https://assets.abfrlcdn.com/js/app/comb/bflyte_desktop/production/userajax.js"></script>

<script type="text/javascript">$('document').ready(function(){$('.menu-container ul.nav li.dropdown').hover(function(){$(".menu_overlay").stop(true,true).fadeIn(250);$(this).find('.dropdown-menu').stop(true,true).fadeIn(300);},function(){$(".menu_overlay").stop(true,true).fadeOut(250);$(this).find('.dropdown-menu').stop(true,true).fadeOut(300);});$('#ViewInventory').click(function(){window.open(strBaseURL+"inventorystatus",'_blank');$.post(strBaseURL+"inventorystatus");});$(".register-tab").click(function(){$(".forgot_password_view").hide();$(".login_existin

g").hide();$(".login_new").show();$(".tabheader").removeClass('active');$(this).addClass('active');$('.login_pop_wrap .err_msg').text('');$(".forgot_password_form_div .help-block").hide();});$(".login-tab").click(function(){$(".forgot_password_view").hide();$(".login_new").hide();$(".login_existing").show();$(".tabheader").removeClass('active');$(this).addClass('active');$('.login_pop_wrap .err_msg').text('');$(".forgot_password_form_div .help-block").hide();});$(".forgot_password").click(function(){$(".tabheader").removeClass('active');});$(".checkout-signup-link").click(function(){$(".tabheader").removeClass('active');$(".register-tab").addClass('active');setTimeout(function(){$(document).find('.modal-backdrop').addClass('OverlayColor');});});$(".login_wrap").click(function(){$(".tabheader").removeClass('active');$(".register-tab").addClass('active');$(".modal-backdrop").addClass('OverlayColor');});$(".modal-backdrop, .login_pop_wrap .modal-dialog button.close").click(function(){$(".modal-backdrop").removeClass('OverlayColor');});if(window.location.href.indexOf("store_code")!==-1){StoreCode=window.location.href.indexOf("store_code=");QueryString=window.location.href.substr(StoreCode,100);arrQueryString=QueryString.split("&");strStoreCodeQueryString=arrQueryString[0];arrQueryString1=strStoreCodeQueryString.split("=");strStoreCode=arrQueryString[0];strStoreName='allensolly';strStoreId=2;customRedirection=strStoreName+'/virtual-store';var dt=new Date();dt.setTime(dt.getTime()+(1000*60*60*24));exp_dt=new

Date(dt).toUTCString();var expires='';
expires="+exp_dt;document.cookie="STORECODE =
"+strStoreCode+expires+"; path=/";document.cookie="STOREBRAND =
"+strStoreName+expires+";
path=/";document.cookie="STOREBRANDID = "+strStoreId+expires+";
path=/";document.cookie="REDIRECTION =
"+customRedirection+expires+";
path=/";window.location.href=strBaseURL+customRedirection;}if(strPag
eName!="category"){setTimeout(function(){bLazy.revalidate();},300);}if(s
trPageName=="product"){$(".web-engagement-
close").on('click',function(){$(this).parent().hide();});}});</script>

<script>if(window.addEventListener){window.addEventListener("messag
e",receive,false);}else{if(window.attachEvent){window.attachEvent("onme
ssage",receive,false);}}function receive(event){var
data=event.data;if(typeof(window[data.func])=="function"){window[data.
func].call(null,data.params[0]);}}function temp(message){var
objProduct=JSON.parse(message);var
intProductID=objProduct.productdetails.mainsku;var
intAttributeID=objProduct.productdetails.config.size_id;var
intQuantity=1;switch(objProduct.actionname){case"Details":window.ope
n(strBaseURL+'product/'+objProduct.productdetails.LinkRewrite+"-
"+objProduct.productdetails.mainsku+".html?size="+objProduct.product
details.config.size,'_blank');break;case"Add To
Cart":TRENDIN.AddToCart(intProductID,intAttributeID,intQuantity,fal
se);break;case"Wishlist":if(!parseInt(isCustomerLoggedIn)){fnLoginRegi

ster();$(document).find('.modal-backdrop').addClass('OverlayColor');$('.login-tab').trigger('click');}else TRENDIN.AddToWishlist(intProductID,intAttributeID);break;case"Buy Now":TRENDIN.AddToCart(intProductID,intAttributeID,intQuantity,true,'','buynow');break;}}</script>

<script type="text/javascript">var intProductID="207096";var imgUrl="https://assets.abfrlcdn.com/img/app/product/2/207096-638641.jpg";var srcvalue="https://vanheusenindia.fitrrati.com/widget/fitwidget?rid=2200225";var controllerpath="vanheusenindiafit/";</script>

<script type="text/javascript" async="true" src="https://assets.abfrlcdn.com/js/app/comb/bflyte_desktop/production/vanheusen_product.js"></script>

<script type="text/javascript">var cartdata=[];</script>

<script type="text/javascript">if(strPageName!="category"){var bLazy=new Blazy({selector:'img',offset:0});$('document').ready(function(){$('.menu-container ul.nav li.dropdown').hover(function(){bLazy.revalidate();},function(){bLazy.revalidate();});});}</script>

<script type="text/javascript">(function($){$.fn.customerPopup=function(e,intWidth,intHeight,blnResize){e.preventDefault();intWidth=intWidth||'500';intHeight=intHeight||'400';strResize=(blnResize?'yes':'no');var

strTitle=((typeof this.attr('title')!=='undefined')?this.attr('title'):'Social Share'),strParam='width='+intWidth+',height='+intHeight+',resizable='+strResize,objWindow=window.open(this.attr('href'),strTitle,strParam).focus();}

$(document).ready(function($){$('.customer.share').on("click",function(e){$(this).customerPopup(e);});});}(jQuery));$('ul.dropdown-menu.mega-dropdown-menu').on('click',function(event){event.stopPropagation();});</script>

<script type="text/javascript">var google_tag_params={ecomm_prodid:207096,ecomm_pagetype:strPageName,ecomm_totalvalue:3499,};</script>

<script type="text/javascript">var google_conversion_id=875926909;var google_custom_params=window.google_tag_params;var google_remarketing_only=true;</script>

<script type="text/javascript" src="//www.googleadservices.com/pagead/conversion.js">

</script>

</body>

</html>

Milton Keynes UK
Ingram Content Group UK Ltd.
UKHW021832031123
431812UK00014B/452